CHILD'S PLAY
'Direct Work' with the Deprived Child

by
Ken Redgrave

PUBLISHED BY THE

BOYS' AND GIRLS' WELFARE SOCIETY

Published by the Boys' and Girls' Welfare Society 1987
Schools Hill, Cheadle, Cheshire SK8 1JE.

Typeset & printed by Manchester Free Press
59 Whitworth Street, Manchester M1 3WT. 061-236 8822.

ISBN 1 869801 03 2

Registered Charity No. 209782

To
SHEILA REDGRAVE
whose warmth and empathy have
helped so many children

Preface

This book is intended to be a practical guide for people who are working with disturbed children and who are involved in what has come to be called 'direct work' with children. However, the underlying philosophy, which stresses the value of a 'good enough' parenting and nurturing experience will, it is hoped, ensure that the book is helpful to people who are interested in child care and development in more general terms.

The helping methods described in this book, often referred to as 'games', may be used when counselling children, when re-alerting or stimulating the senses or providing regression experiences, and when assessing a child's psychological and social needs. Many of the *games* were devised in order to make the communication of ideas and feelings flow more easily between child and adult.

During the past ten years the demand for people to help children in accordance with the methods described in the book has grown apace. Training courses have been run in most of the Social Services departments and some people have begun to specialize in *direct work*. Various categories of workers, including Guardians ad Litem, are finding it necessary to develop expertise in communicating with children, and helping withdrawn or hostile children to communicate with them. Often this need is related to court work. In my own teaching experience I am frequently asked for printed material and 'hand-outs' which will illustrate the methods I have been using and telling students about. This book is intended to do that. It draws not only on my own ideas but on ideas thought up by other practitioners and which have now become more widely used.

There are a few observations I would like to include in this preface. First, the book as it stands does not attempt to provide a theory of child counselling or psychotherapy. In the main it describes various 'Third Objects' (*games*) and activities. For anyone using these *third objects* in connection with in-depth counselling or therapy work, a thorough knowledge of child psychology and child development and of course counselling methods, are necessary. But the *third objects* themselves may be used at any level and by people who have very different roles one from another.

Second, it is important to emphasize that many children will not be ready, when first referred for help, to make use of the more directed (i.e. focussed) activities which many of the *third-objects* imply. Such children may first require a period (i.e. several sessions) where they are allowed free-play and where the main objective of the worker might be to provide the sort of sensory experiences discussed in Chapter Four of the book. In any case I usually give a free-choice free-play period in each session, even though other parts of the session might be *focussed* (a word I prefer to 'directed').

Third, in making use of the methods spoken about in the book it is important that workers should be aware of the *interactive* process involved in the development of personality. It is not only what the parent does *to* the child, it is also what the child does to the parent, or less specifically, the environment's influence on the child and the child's influence on its environment.

Lastly, let me emphasize that the book is intended as a guide, and only as a guide. It would be quite wrong for anyone to issue a working pack for people who wished to undertake *direct work*, and to provide sets of questionnaire cards and things of that sort. In my practice, and that of my colleagues, the *games* are being constantly adapted to the needs of the individual child. I have attempted to provide *examples* and to state a few principles, but each worker must draw upon his or her imagination and make up new *games*. In any case, we all bring different personalities to the work. Some, for example, may find it easy to play-act with young children whilst others couldn't do that easily. I see this work as very much an art to which we bring our individuality and imagination.

Throughout the book I use both masculine and feminine personal pronouns, sometimes referring to she/*her* and at other times to *he*/his. To me this seems more natural than sticking all the way through to one or the other.

Descriptions of children and adults in this book, although drawn from similar people found in my case notes, do not describe actual individuals, child or adult. I have used oft repeated situations and circumstances, and where I have described case-histories or parts of case-histories, I have drawn from many others, which are similar. Where I have had particular children in mind I have disguised the circumstances (such as age, sex, place and time) without doing violence to the psychological reality of the child or the family described.

KEN REDGRAVE

Acknowledgements

I would like to acknowledge Sally Gething for her scrutiny and advice, and both Sheila Redgrave and Edith Westerman for their typing at various stages.

I also acknowledge Pat Owen and Pat Curtis for allowing reproductions from 'Techniques for Working with Children: 1', and Basil Blackwell Publishers and Dr. Fitzgerald for allowing reproductions from 'Building New Families' by John Fitzgerald and Brenda & Bill Murcer.

KEN REDGRAVE

Foreword

This is the second in a new series of texts on current social and educational caring issues published by the Boys' and Girls' Welfare Society.

The series addresses topics of interest and concern to a wide range of professional carers including social workers, teachers, psychologists, psychiatrists, administrators, managers and frequently parents.

Children should have the absolute right to a happy childhood and be able to grow up in an environment which fosters their development towards becoming stable, well adjusted and caring adults. Unfortunately, all too often this is not the case and many children exhibit difficult and disturbed behaviour as a result of their personal circumstances. Such children need special help and attention.

Ken Redgrave has been helping difficult and disturbed children for many years and has become synonymous with the method referred to as 'direct work'.

This essentially practical and informative guide will prove invaluable to all those involved in dealing with disturbed children and young people.

JOHN McG. McMASTER
Chief Executive
Boys' And Girls' Welfare Society

Contents

Chapter One

A Tree Called Jamie

Jamie

Perhaps one day I shall write the full story of Jamie. If I do it will bear the title of 'A Tree called Jamie'. This is because one of the last games we played before he went to his new family involved a tree which grew up. But let me tell you the story in brief:

Jamie was eight when I first met him. I had read about him, and had been asked by the Local Authority in whose care he had been placed to:-

 a). Prepare Jamie for long-term placement.
 b). Select and prepare a new family for him.
 c). Place him, and maintain support once he was placed.

Jamie was in a Children's Home run by a voluntary society. For most of his childhood this little boy had drifted. A sad and disturbing story emerged as I read his case-file. Here was an intelligent but bewildered child. A child who had enjoyed no feelings of deep down security. No feelings of permanency so far as any family was concerned. People shook their heads at the idea of finding a foster family for Jamie. Jamie was not fosterable — and certainly not adoptable.

The file said:

'Jamie was received into care six times during his first two years of life, sometimes with injuries, and given away to a neighbour on one occasion by his mother who felt unable to cope.
When he was three he was placed with foster parents, the Stanards. He left them when six years old as they could cope no longer. He is described as doubly incontinent, aggressive, abusive, manipulative and non-responsive to love'.

Jamie had moved from place to place. Quite often in between moves he'd been placed back home into the care of his mother and her current co-habitee. I counted seventeen moves in his eight-year-old life, including the times he went back home. Just before I met him at *Greenlawns*, the Children's Home, he had spent his final period at home, a period which lasted only six weeks. Again, the file said:

'so Jamie returned home. He ran away eight times and after about six weeks was received into care again and placed in *Greenlawns*.'

Jamie's story is far more detailed and in some ways more shocking than I can relate here, but the few facts I have given will help readers to understand why it was that he was so mixed up, so aggressive, and so deprived. He didn't really know the feel of a secure family, nor how to interact with others. Nor did he understand the normal roles of parents, and I'm not surprised. Even the first two years of his life were surprisingly complicated:

At six months	hospital, serious extensive bruising. Received into care for one month,
At nine months	placed with a friend 'for keeps'.
At ten months	received into public care, foster home.
At one year	hospital, hairline fracture of the skull. Received into care for three months.
At eighteen months	public care for two months.
At one year nine months	public care overnight, 'left alone'.
At two years	public care, foster home. Mother felt stepfather might injure child.

In the following chapters I shall describe a number of games I used in helping Jamie. I wanted to find out how he saw his past, and what fantasies he had about it. I wanted to know how he felt about people in his life.

Children who have been deprived often carry fantasies which make it impossible for them to accept new families or even to integrate with their natural family.

But children don't like being questioned about their feelings, especially by people who may start off with the disadvantage of being strangers to them. They may experience us as dangerous, or embarrassing, or just meaningless. That's why I use so many games.

I feel that helping children, especially when they are requiring a family, is like setting off on a magic carpet adventure. I may not at the start know the route for the journey — the itinerary. I seldom know what the end of the journey will be. A magic carpet is not like a bridge. A bridge is firm, solid, and it goes from point 'A' to point 'B'. It's all worked out. But this sort of work with children is different. The magic carpet goes up and down. It can be a bit scary at times for me as well as the child, and we never quite know which direction the carpet will take.

As Jamie and I had never met, I started by writing a letter to him. Of course he'd been told I was coming to see him and that I wanted to talk about finding a family for him. Other people had been talking with him about these matters.Jamie liked the idea of a letter arriving especially for him. I wrote it in my best copper-plate handwriting and chose the words carefully. In fact he is quite a bright child so it was easy to communicate in this way.

Early in our relationship I arrived with an empty box file. The sort of thing used in an office. The idea, I told Jamie, was for us to put as many Jamie things as we could find into the empty box. Especially we needed to find photographs of himself and members of his family — I'd made sure he was given some early pictures of himself and family a week or so before our first meeting — so when I produced the box Jamie ran upstairs to his bedroom and returned with his offering.

When we are doing these things it helps the child to converse if some con-structing, sticking, cutting or painting exercise is going on. We then avoid what I call the *interview situation*. I suppose we are often using a *third object*, in this case the box, in order to communicate more easily.

So, since the box was just plain on its outside, Jamie was able to put his name on the lid. You can have fun just doing that. You don't have to *write* it. A child can paint it, crayon it, or colour in the letters the adult has drawn. But another real fun thing is to use the modern dry transfer letters you just rub onto the writing surface.

Children like to use symbolism. Often when discussing their drawings or paintings symbolism comes in. They tell me that the big black cloud they've painted is angry, or that the trees are happy like they themselves were when they lived with Auntie Mabel

'How d'you know the trees are happy?'
'Because they are holding hands'

The branches were touching. The empty box, I explained, was like me in that I did not really know what it was to be like Jamie. Perhaps he had angry feelings and happy feelings. If we talked then perhaps he could 'fill me in' with his feelings. Also, I needed to know about the things he could remember. Like the box, I needed filling up with information.

This book is full of 'games' and other activities in which symbolism plays an important part. When working with children in the way I am describ-ing we *must* be aware of the constant stream of signals we and the children are sending. Often the signals are expressed in symbolic form, perhaps in drawing or painting or by means of an object or a piece of role-play, and of course in the dreams children may tell you about.

It is important that, when you design 'games' or involve yourself in role-play, all your imagination faculty should be awake to the use of symbolism both by yourself and the child. You should develop not only the 'third ear' described by Winnicott (1964) by means of which you 'hear' something in addition to the straight verbal message, but a third eye that will 'see' what others may miss.

Most people who work with children have heard about Life Story Books. These have been around for several years now. I shall discuss them in greater detail later in this book.

I felt Jamie needed a Life Story Book. Or to be more precise, he needed a life story experience. The book itself is one thing, the experience of making it and talking about the photographs and other memorabilia (birthday cards, letters, etc.), is quite another.

However, Jamie's life had been so mixed up, even though he was only eight, and there had been so many moves that I felt he needed to be able to get a pictorial view of it, all stretched out in a line before him so to speak, before we began making a Life Story Book.

So we played the game of flow charts. I've included specimens of these further on in the book. The idea is that important stages in the child's life are described and different moves, addresses and so forth, are written down and strung out in a line. Jamie and I worked on one of these for about three months. He used to have this pinned up on the wall in his bedroom. We used it to help us sort out where he'd come from and where he might be going to. It was something that he lived with for all these months. Sometimes conversation would go like this:

'When you went home that time, Jamie, was that when Bill was your stepfather?'.
'No, Bill was in prison, I think he was — I think he beat me mum up'.
'Who was your dad at that time, because you said you could remember three dads?'.
'Trevor, it was Trevor, I didn't like him — I'll put his name in down here'.
'O.K. you put his name in — what colour?'.
'Black'.
'Why black?'.
'Don't know (here Jamie began using the black felt tip pen) — I think it's because black's horrible — Trevor used the belt on me'.
'Did your sisters get the belt too?'.
'Nope — only me'.
'Would you like to go home to your sisters?'.
'No, I'd go home without them, but not with them'.

It was whilst using the flow chart that Jamie was able to say that he felt going home again would not work. Remember, despite the description the case file gave of him, he was an intelligent boy and with help, using the games, he could reach wise conclusions about realities in situations. It was important, however 'bad' his parents were, that I was not seen by him as a person coming in full of disgust and rejection towards them.

I had been seeing Jamie for four months before he was able to let me know quite firmly that he wanted me to find a family for him as soon as

I could. I devised other games for talking about the kind of family he might fit into. There was one game I can remember particularly well concerning Jamie. I called it What is a Family? and the whole idea was to set up opportunities for me to get Jamie talking about and thinking about family life as it should be, not as he'd experienced it. This was a difficult thing to achieve with an eight year old boy, even one as intelligent as Jamie. This game is also illustrated and discussed elsewhere in this book but, briefly, it involved Jamie in drawing, crayoning, cutting out and sticking, and most important discussing certain questions about family life; what 'dads' were supposed to do, what 'mums' were supposed to do, and how they might be expected to react to children's behaviour.

Most of the discussion, or talk, about family life went on while Jamie was engaged in the creative activities described above. The 'board' we played this game on, a large sheet of paper in reality measuring about one and a half metres square, had spaces for our answers to be written in. Sometimes, if Jamie was heavily engaged, I'd write in his answers. Sometimes he would write them in himself.

The time came when we had found a couple who appeared to be right for Jamie, which also meant he was right for them. There followed a series of introduction sessions when he stayed with them, first just for half a day, then later a whole weekend, then a whole week during the school midterm holiday.

The time factor for this transfer process can be quite critical and is discussed elsewhere. People find that all sorts of tensions arise if it is stretched into months. On the other hand, as may happen in any aspect of child care work, we sometimes run up against factors which are beyond our immediate control. In Jamie's case, for example, I felt that it was particularly important that Jamie should be able to finish his school day when he went to his new family, and be welcomed home by one of his new parents. The Glovers were both working but Michelle Glover always intended to stop work, at least for a time, if she took a foster child. However, she was contracted to three months' notice and for various reasons had to stick to the contract. It was necessary therefore to extend the introductory period to cover the three months.

It was then that I thought up the idea of *Trees*. This game was intended to serve a double purpose. It would serve to give Jamie an idea of the time factor involved since a four month period was mapped out on the 'board', overlapping into the time he would be actually placed with the Glovers. At the beginning of each month he had to cut out and stick into place — a tree. But these trees were symbolic representations of Jamie, and the main thing was to see how large and firm the roots were growing. Jamie and I had looked at a plant growing in a pot in *Greenlawns*, and I'd explained that I wanted him to be able to join onto the new family, to grow roots, just like that plant had done in the plant pot. It was so firmly in that you could pick up the plant and the pot would come too!

Jamie used to stay with the Glovers each weekend and again at mid-term. He and I would talk about how things had gone with him and the Glovers. They were also involved in sessions where we all had something to say about how things had gone.

When we played *Trees* we always started off with a root formation larger than the previous Tree. If there had been difficulties or 'naughty' tantrums we saw these as things which got at the roots of our tree and I would snip off a bit of the root formation with the scissors — not too much — I didn't wish to dishearten him!

By the time the three months were up Jamie was ready to move permanently into his new family, there was a stout tree with extensive root formation. We pointed to it and said, 'that's a tree called Jamie'. Of course Jamie and the Glovers had a lot of adjustments to make. There were to be many things which got at the roots over the following year or two. But, four years on, he is not only happily settled with the Glovers but is looking forward to being legally adopted soon. Jamie really has flowered into a child who has overcome the trauma of earlier times and events.

Wendy

'How about sticking a coloured square on for your Mummy?'

'I don't want to'.

'You'd rather not, eh? Are you sure? What about a yellow one, she'd like yellow?'

''No, I don't want to'.

Pause — silence for a while

'Why not?'

'It makes me sad'.

This was part of a conversation I had once with Wendy when she was just seven and a half years old. Wendy and I were playing a very special game. As you see, there were some parts which were sad about this game.

About a year before this, her mother had separated from 'dad' who was Wendy's stepfather, and had gone to live with another man called Joe. At that time Wendy and Joe were like oil and water, they didn't blend easily. So it was a choice for Wendy's mum — Joe or Wendy? She chose Joe, and in a round about way Wendy went into public care.

The Juvenile Court made an Order committing her to the care of the local authority. She spent a few months in a Children's Home where it was decided she should be placed with a couple who wanted to adopt a little girl — the Ormrods.

It was about this time that I met her, just as she was about to move into the Ormrods. They had a lovely little cottage but they were not cottagers. They were nice people, intelligent, sophisticated, professional.

It didn't work. Wendy was miserable in the lovely modernised cottage. And even though her mother had seemingly abandoned her, Wendy still thought about her. She also longed to be with her grandparents or her 'dad' and two younger brothers. But 'dad' had also gone off with another woman who wouldn't have Wendy. In fact nobody in her family was prepared to care for her. Her mother wrote to her and said:

'My darling, darling Wendy — I love you *very* much and I do mean very much. I can't say just how I feel because it is hard to know how to say it but we had to do something because I couldn't stand it any longer so none of us was happy. I don't think they should have taken you away like that, but now it's happened I suppose it will all be for the best. Sorry I had to disappear but that is how Joe wanted it. He won't let me have you but I still love you and one day when you are grown up you will understand, so be a good girl and cheer up. Love to you and love to Nan and Grandad if you see them. I love you, I love you.

Mum

xxxxx

xxx

The local authority also had a letter from Wendy's mother in which she said she now agreed that adoption would be a good thing for Wendy.

But Wendy had other ideas. She had in fact said 'yes' when the staff members asked if she wanted to go and live with the Ormrods, though not at first. First she had hopes that she could go to her Nan's and Grandad. She loved them, and Grandad really spoilt her. Or maybe back to 'dad' and his new wife — she could easily learn to call her 'mum'.

Later on, however, she said 'yes' to going to the Ormrods. Staff said she couldn't stay there in the Children's Home because it was only for 'short-term'. Wendy was unhappy about that because she liked it there and at the day school, Hepworth Primary. Also, staff and her social worker said she couldn't go to Nan's or to 'Dad's. They were in fact telling her the truth. All her relations said they couldn't cope. So in the end she had to say 'yes' and she was placed with the Ormrods.

She ran away several times, taking off early in the morning usually, and creeping out of the house before the Ormrods were up. A desperate Pauline Ormrod would ring me up.

Wendy made her feelings known in other ways. Whenever the Ormrods took her to buy new clothes — and they bought her some fahtastic outfits — she showed them up in the stores, and if the store assistant said 'Your mummy won't be pleased' she shouted back — yes, *shouted* — 'she's not my mummy. I've got my own mummy'. This was very painful for Pauline Ormrod who wanted people to feel nice about her little girl and who'd been thinking about having a little girl for quite a time. She also wanted them to like her nice clothes and her lovely manners.

On one occasion Wendy agreed to show me her new clothes so I went upstairs and peeped into her wardrobe and there I saw some really fantastic frocks, two-piece suits, and a super fashionable coat. As I was exclaiming about these lovely things and actually lifting some of them out, I noticed that she was much more interested in what looked like a jumble sale all spread out on her bed. 'Come and look at *these*' she said. So I did. 'These' were the clothes she owned before she came to the Ormrods. In fact quite a few of them were the ones she'd worn at home — and a motley collection they made.

The conversation we had which introduced this section was part of a game we were playing — but this came along a bit later and is explained in detail later on in this book. What we had to do was to paste a picture of Wendy in the middle of a board and then to paste coloured squares of paper around her. These coloured squares had names on them. They were the names of all the pople she wanted to talk about with me, or maybe she'd like to draw pictures about them instead of talking. Or maybe I could go and see them and talk about her to them. She came up with several names. She put a beautiful green square on for Nan and Grandad, and a blue one for her 'dad' and brothers. Also she wanted a square stuck on for the teachers at Hepworth Primary and one for the staff at the Children's Home.

After this we joined all these coloured squares up with Wendy simply by drawing lines leading from the squares back to her picture — a bit like a spider's web with a cute spider in the middle. She decided to make the whole thing much prettier so she painted coloured ribbons or streamers leading back to herself, then added flowers and dots so that in the end it was marvellous.

I remember another game we played — mail boxes or post boxes. Wendy sometimes felt shy about bringing up a subject she wanted to talk about, but I noticed that on a few occasions before we thought up the game she would go away quietly and scribble something down on a scrap of paper, hand it to me and then dash off and engage in some energetic activity such as handstands or cartwheels. These little notes said things like 'want to tork abowt crying'. So we were able to talk about this. If she hadn't written it down we could have missed it. Therefore we made a mail box. She enjoyed making it. We covered it with coloured wrapping paper and made a slit for notes to be posted and mailed to me, and a door in the side so that I could get any notes out. I used to open it whenever I visited her.

The point about these games was that they made it easier for me and Wendy to talk about things — things that are often very difficult to talk about. In the long run, too, we both knew much more about her and her feelings. We also knew more about why other people had acted in the way they did, and Wendy began to learn about how things really were in her life. I felt this would help her when it came to working out the future.

The time came when we had to move her from the Ormrods and put her in another Children's Home. As so often happens, the Homes I wanted to use were full and she finished up in a place where the staff did their best but were not geared to a child of her age — most of the others were teenagers.

This move gave me a chance, however. Wendy had been wrongly placed previously. There were so many features which should have warned decision-making staff against placing her for adoption, and many more which should have ruled out the Ormrods as a match for her. Now we had a chance to find out much more about her and to involve her in preparation for future care. This meant that I had to work directly with the child. Already she had strong negative feelings about foster parents — any foster parents. She was becoming equally disillusioned with Children's Homes and hated the place she had now moved to.

Wendy was in danger of becoming a good specimen of the deprived child with a chip on her shoulder and given to anti-social behaviour. She had to be helped, and she had to help us to discover her inner self and her real needs. To do this I needed to be really in touch with her, and she needed to be able to express all her fears so that we could help to remove them. Then we had to have confidence in one another so that the future placement, wherever that might be, would meet her needs. Perhaps, also, she needed to make some adjustments in order to fit into other people's lives.

We had some really good families as possible families for her, but she would see none of them. One day she told me that she liked places where the houses 'were all cosy together' — all near each other. So I got her to paint a picture of such 'cosy' houses. As she painted she talked. Another time she painted a picture of a house that was sad — it was lonely. We talked about these houses and gave them names. The houses talked to one another. One house was Wendy when she was sad — the cottage on its own — and one house, squashed in between others, was Wendy when she was happy and secure.

She got into trouble at school and at the Home, and on one occasion when she went to a party. I remember a game we played at that time. We played it in between more ordinary games with dolls and dolls' houses. In this game I made a whole set of cards, in fact several sets. Each set had a different coloured border. The Blue border was for things to do with school; the Red bordered cards were about things to do with the Home; and the Yellow bordered cards were to do with her own family. On some of the cards I wrote short statements. For example, on the school cards we have "Teachers" or "Other children"; on the family cards we had "My Mummy" or "Going back to my family" and so on. We played at taking turns to choose a subject to talk about, or draw a picture about, or to act a story about, using a doll's house and toy people. This game helped me to learn about Wendy's attitudes and it gave me the opportunity to give her ideas about how she might do better with people at school or in the Home. It also gave me and Wendy an opportunity to show feelings about her being in care and the reality of 'going home'.

Wendy's story is a long one. It would fill a book. I have known her now for four years. In the following chapters of this book a lot of games will be illustrated and a few ideas thrown in. It was ideas such as these, and games like these, which helped me to help Wendy and her family. Now at the age of eleven and a half she is a responsive, happy, outgoing child, doing well at school and living with her mother. It is now nearly two years since she was returned to her mother.

Daniel.

Daniel is seven. He was greatly attached to his father who died eighteen months ago as a result of a serious road accident. Shortly afterwards his mother deserted the family — Daniel, his sister a year older than him, and Wilfred now aged five.

He had never been accepted by his large extended family on his mother's side, who saw his father in him, whilst the other children were seen as reflecting all the characteristics of the mother. Even Daniel's mother used to tell him that he would grow up 'just like your father' — meaning a very nasty and undesirable person. But was Daniel's father a nasty and undesirable person? Daniel loved him. Did Daniel have deep down feelings that he should not have loved him because he was 'nasty'? Worse still, did Daniel feel a deep down sense of guilt about his dad dying in a motor car crash? Was he, Daniel, in some way to blame? Why did he paint all those pictures? — actually they were not much more than scribbles but he said they were pictures of motor cars running Daniel over.

At first Daniel and his siblings went into a short-term foster home maintained by the local authority. *Short-term* it was called, but months went by and the children came to feel they might stay there. They didn't know for certain of course. This was bad because they developed all sorts of feelings of insecurity.

Then the family took the other two children out of care, but they wouldn't have Daniel who was too much like his father. Soon after this the short-term foster mother became ill so Daniel went to another 'short-term' foster home. It might have been better to have used a Children's Home right from the start, but just at this time when Daniel was in care Children's Homes were out of fashion and short-term foster homes were back in. He became even more disturbed. His behaviour at school was difficult. If checked, especially by the auxiliary staff (canteen staff for instance) he would use obscene expressions about where they should go and what they should do with themselves.

He ruined other children's games. This happened in the foster home. If he didn't win he would smash the whole thing up. He had no idea of time and if allowed to play out until five in the evening would disappear and turn up at seven o'clock.

Daniel was a little boy who showed many signs of deprivation. When we made a closer study of him and got the foster parents to help in an assessment we found that we were dealing with a child who, in many respects, was like a four or five-year-old. Some bits of his behaviour were even those of a two-year-old. But in his case, as with many deprived children, it was very easy to miss out on this and see him as 'normal but naughty and wilful'. Of course he *was* naughty, and he was wilful, just like four-year-olds or two-year-olds are *before we have nurtured and trained them to other ways and they have developed inner control.*

Daniel was not mentally handicapped in the normal sense of the term. He was not even mildly educationally sub-normal. That expression usually refers to some built-in or innate limitation. His main problem was *emotional* retardation, not so much intellectual.

Daniel, like many deprived children, had not developed an inner control over his emotional impulses. Two-year-olds have temper tantrums easily and frequently. So do many deprived, *emotionally* deprived, older children. Many emotionally disturbed and socially deprived young children behave as if they have lost the ability to *experience* things as people usually do. They often cannot 'understand' or, to use a more technical term, they cannot *conceptualise* easily. Daniel could not understand time in terms of days or weeks. He used to get his days mixed up and then both he and his foster parents became worked up when they tried to teach him.

So what games did I play with him? He needed to be able to go over, in his mind, the terrible hurts that had happened to him. He needed to be able to feel good about the dad he loved. He needed to be able to express the angry feelings inside himself.

This problem of time and days and weeks, for example. It was really only a side issue but it was causing extra little frustrations so I devised a game of help Daniel. Like many of my other games this one is described elsewhere in this book. Briefly, it was a card marked out in days and weeks. Each week had seven small squares (6 x 6 cmts.) set out in a row — Monday to Sunday - from left to right. The squares were left blank but each day Daniel had to fill one in. Just the one, the *appropriate* one, for that day. In the square he drew a symbol representing the weather.

I supplied him with a set of symbols to copy. For example, on a wet day he copied a simple picture of an umbrella (what matter if he drew mushrooms rather than umbrellas!). On a clear sunny day a big round sun with lines radiating outward, and on a windy day — a windmill. Daniel also had a little cut-out paper boy representing himself. Each day he moved himself on to the appropriate day. The days had colours. Mondays were drawn in red lines, Tuesdays in green, and so on. It was interesting to see just how quickly he began to get the idea of the correct sequence of days, and the idea of a whole week. It took about six weeks for a great improvement to show up. Remember, he was a deprived child, but basically of normal intelligence.

Daniel wanted to visit his father's grave. He wanted not to forget him. He also wanted to remember nice things about him. We made a special 'My Dad' box which he painted after we'd stuck white paper round it. Then he wrote out, or rather I wrote out, on little pieces of card all sorts of memories:

'My dad used to take me fishing'
'My dad used to tickle me'
'Dad used to cook chips sometimes'.

We also played with soft, squashy, coloured *Play-doh,* ideal for three or four year olds! But we also played football. As you see Daniel is a mixture. One day he said he would make some *Play-doh* faces. He flattened out the material and made one face 'nice', smiling, and one face 'nasty', with a crushed mouth:

'Who's that you've made, Daniel — the one who is nasty?'
'It's my Mum, I hate her'.
'Why?'
'She went off — I hate her'.
'She might come back — perhaps she's got troubles — perhaps she was so upset about your dad. What would you do if she came back?'
'I'd do this......'

Then he hit the *Play-doh* face of his mother and squashed it flat.

This action led on to our talking about his mother and looking at photographs. Sometimes it is not a matter of correcting wrong impressions. Certainly we found things which were happy to remember about Daniel's mother. I tried to help him find these memories. But he needed to be able to talk to someone about the wrong things done to him.

So in these games I may help a child to get a *new* and historically true picture of past events, but at other times I am sharing thoughts on events which really, were 'unfair', 'unkind' or 'unfortunate'.

I have talked about playing *games* with children. The main thing about these 'games' is that they enabled a child and an adult to say something to each other. They made it possible for children to learn about themselves, their past, their feelings and their possible future experiences. The methods and devices used helped me to learn much more about the children and their misconceptions, anger, fears and wishes.

Direct work of this sort, if used sensitively and with an understanding of the developmental process in children and young people, has been found to be important, if not crucial, in preparing them for major moves and changes in their lives, especially when the child to be moved has experienced social and emotional deprivation. 'Direct Work' here means a direct involvement with the child, as distinct from advice or counselling which may be offered by a professional worker to other adults who are caring for the child. This book is about direct work.

This book concentrates on the use of direct work in the preparation of children for major life changes. This includes work with certain severely deprived young children who have lost the ability to experience even sensory stimulation. That is to say, children who may need to relearn what it is to taste, or to experience smell, or 'hot'/'cold' feeling. Such children often need an enriched nurturing experience built into the direct work programme, what Judith Morris calls *Re-alerting the senses* (1987). They may need *regressive nurturing* experiences which allow them to act our in controlled situations as if they were much younger than their chronological ages.

A distinction needs to be made between 'free- (or 'non-focussed') play' and 'focussed-play'. In Chapters Two and Three the emphasis will be on work (or play!) which has the objective of helping child and worker to focus on certain aspects of life. The techniques described are therefore, to some extent, 'directive'. In Chapter Four the need for free-play is referred to. Many children, particularly those who are severely deprived or disturbed, will need to make use of a free-play, non-focussed approach *first* before the more focussed approaches are used.

Chapter Two

Communicating with Children — Techniques, Methods, Equipment

As we've seen in Chapter One, when we are preparing an already deprived child for a further move we may need to learn what feelings he has about deeply personal life experiences. These may be experiences which have wounded the child emotionally and may have resulted in feelings of loss and anger.

The child may hold very mixed or ambivalent attitudes about the natural parents or about previous caregivers (foster parents, staff of homes, etc). He may long for the return of a parent and at the same time carry feelings of resentment against the same parent for having deserted or ill-treated him. Apart from uncovering these attitudes and helping the child to express feelings and to resolve certain intellectual and emotional problems, we may also consider it necessary to help him at least to begin to 'see things in a different light'.

There have been times when I have wanted a child to begin to develop new ideas about life experiences which we all take for granted and yet I found it very difficult to put into words the aim of the exercise. For example, I wanted Jamie to begin to think about families in a different way. In brief, I wanted to be able to talk with him about the *value* of a child to a family. These are difficult areas even for adults to think about. Putting it technically, I wanted to help him develop new concepts. That was why I invented the game 'What is a family?'

Of course, he would have to experience a new family and 'live the part' before he could really change. But in order to use the mistakes and the misunderstandings and frustrations he and his new parents might experience during the period of introduction and grafting, Jamie and I had to start looking at families and at what was expected of dads and mums and children.

In this chapter I shall introduce and explain some of the 'games' used in order to facilitate discussion and to help children express feelings. Quite often we have to help children to face up to difficult matters if we want to avoid their building up ideas which are unhelpful and are likely to cause pain, if not disruption, later on.

It is not always easy, for example, to help a child learn about the reasons why she has never been cared for by her own mother. Yet the ideas she holds, which bear no resemblance to historical facts, may prevent her ever settling with anybody or ever having positive relationships. Nor is it easy for a child to tell an adult just how she feels about these matters, yet if pressed she may say something, anything, to get herself out of a painful or embarrassing interview situation. I used that expression 'interview situation' deliberately because I wanted to stress that when this direct work is undertaken no child should feel he is in such a situation. If children do feel they are being interviewed there is something wrong with our approach or technique, and it is very unlikely that meaningful messages will be either given or received by child or adult. Some form of communication may go on, but it may have as much to do with *hiding* ideas as with transmitting them.

Before introducing examples of special games or devices let me stress that many ordinary everyday objects and activities can and should be used in direct work with children. The use of these ordinary objects and activities may seem elementary but nevertheless they are often overlooked, and yet people who want to do this work with children need to develop a flair for thinking up all sorts of ways of turning them into useful *third objects*.

'Third Object'.

Imagine you are making a visit to a mother and her young child of eighteen months or two years of age. This is the first time you have called to see them. The child does not know you. Has never seen you before. When you go into the room and sit down he runs and clambers up on the mother's lap or stands holding on to her. The mother says she will make some coffee and goes through to the kitchen. The child follows her. A little later you are chatting with the mother who has returned with the coffee. You haven't ignored the child's presence. Maybe you've looked in his direction, smiled, said "Hello". Maybe you've picked up a toy that was lying on the floor, admired it and put it down again. All the time the child is watching you. Gradually he leaves his mother's lap and moves a few feet from her. He feels safe. He plays with some of his toys.

Then something special happens. The child walks over to you and hands you a toy truck. He uses no words. You admire the truck. 'What a lovely red truck — and look, there's a yellow one over there'. The child comes over again and takes the red truck from you. He picks up the yellow truck and gives it to you.

Soon you and this rather timid child (there are different types!) are talking to one another. Soon he is beside you. He has left the immediate safety of mother and he is learning about you. This little encounter demonstrates the child's use of a *Third Object* in order to establish communication with you. He's already established that you are 'safe' (even though he's got no word for that). He wanted also to establish a rapport. In a way the toy trucks became an extension of himself. He established a rapport by the use of objects, of media (toys). We have called this *Media Contact* or *Third Object Communication.*

In a moment I shall give a brief analysis (a list of aims) to show the way our games or third objects may be used in direct work with children. Before doing so I would like to give a quote from Violet Oaklander (1978) where she talks about her goal in this sort of work:

> "My goal is to help the child become aware of herself and her existence in her world. Each therapist will find his or her own style in achieving that delicate balance between directing and guiding the session on the one hand, and going with and following the child's lead on the other. The suggestions presented here are intended merely to show you the endless possibilities and to free your own creative process. They are not meant to be followed mechanically."

I think the most important phrase used in this quotation is to be found in the words "......to free your own creative process". My own goal is not to give the reader a rigid prescription or set of prescriptions, or a 'pack' with a set of rules, but to introduce him or her to the 'endless possibilities' which exist for helping children by the use of the third object and by the use of 'child's play'.

It is possible to categorise the 'games' or third objects according to the way these are used in direct work, but I would stress that although a particular device is used especially to obtain or impart a certain kind of information, usually because of the nature of direct work, other information is also being passed (both ways) at the same time. I may, for example, be using a game to tell a child about her earlier life history, where she lived, how old she was, etc., but find that I am learning something about her *feelings* towards these people and events. She is passing this information to me. This sort of overlap is nearly always present in the work. Here is a list showing the different aims I have when using the games and objects in my work:

a). **STARTERS.**
Techniques, situations, or scenarios being used mainly to 'pave the way', 'oil the works', or as we say 'break the ice' and so make it easier to start work with the child.

b). **FOCUSSING ON LIFE TRAIL.**
Techniques used mainly to help the child and me in discussing the child's life trail from birth to present, or in seeing how relationships

stand, or appear to the child to stand, at a particular time in his or her life.

c). **BARRIER-BREAKING.**
Techniques used mainly to help the child and me to break through the barrier which is so often created when children and adults are trying to use *words* for communicating or where the child (or adult) feels embarrassed or shy.

d). **DISCUSSION-DIRECTING.**
Techniques used to help me and the child to direct the discussion along certain paths.

e). **CLARIFYING SOCIAL AND PSYCHO-SOCIAL ASPECTS.**
Techniques used mainly for the child and me to clarify certain social or psycho-social relationships.

f). **FOCUSSING ON FEELINGS.**
Techniques used mainly to help the child and me to discover and talk about his or her feelings such as anxiety, likes, dislikes, anger and so forth. In more technical terms, to talk about 'affective' experiences.

g). **BEHAVIOUR-CHANGE.**
Techniques used mainly to help the child and me to observe, talk about, and if necessary begin to change his or her ways of responding to other people, or interacting with others.

h). **NURTURE.**
Techniques used mainly to provide the child with sensory experiences. That is to say experiences of touch, sound, colour, smell, taste, movement, etc., in order to remedy certain nurturing deficiencies.

i). **PLANNING.**
Techniques used mainly to help the child and me to *plan together* for his or her future.

The first four (a-d) of these categories will be discussed fully in this chapter. The other categories will be briefly illustrated in this chapter but discussed fully in Chapters Three and Four.

STARTERS.

I have already introduced two examples of starters in Chapter One. I mentioned the not very original idea of sending a note to a child by way of introducing oneself. Residential workers already living with a child obviously wouldn't need that sort of starter if they were given the task of undertaking the direct work. Perhaps, however, we may see more residential workers undertaking direct work with children who are in their own homes, then they may need that kind of introduction.

I also introduced the box file idea in Chapter One when I was telling you about Jamie. This is now illustrated in Figure 1. I have already referred to

FIG. 1

David Roberts

An ordinary 'box file' used in preparation.

its value as a third object, especially if the child is encouraged to put his name on or draw a picture on the front. I mentioned also the way an object such as a box file may come to symbolise something. In the case of Jamie I said the box was like me, but of course it could symbolise Jamie, for both of us needed 'filling up' with information.

Notice, however, that Jamie was able to gather a set of early photographs and to put them in the box himself. Jamie, I said, returned with 'his offering'. It is very important that children should be able to *make a contribution* in some way or other in any direct work or planning connected with our helping them. As far as possible we should encourage in the child the feeling of active participation in bringing about a change in his or her life.

Notice also the way the box file, the third object, is used to help bring about what I call a *deflected* discussion. That is to say a discussion goes on about any particular aspect of the child's life although attention *seems to be* on the box. Whilst the child is colouring in his name he is far more likely to answer some question about his father or his own anger than if we are just sitting talking in an interview.

Ordinary things, objects such as telephones, tape recorders, dice games and so on make useful third objects as starters. I often select a piece of 'equipment' which I see as aiding my communication with a particular child — perhaps I'll never use that object with any other child. Sometimes this is because I have previously learned something about the child, something I have been told by the caregivers or I've culled from the case file, and so I've arranged something around the particular object.

Sometimes I have found it helpful as a starter to be able to 'plug in' on some area of special interest or a hobby. The case of Peter, a twelve-year-old boy, illustrates the way in which I was able both to 'plug in' on an interest and to use an ordinary object — a dice football game.

Peter was referred to me when his long-standing foster home was disrupting. The foster parents were unable to talk with him concerning very strong negative feelings he had towards them, nor could he talk with them. Unfortunately, events had made it difficult for his own social worker to communicate with Peter on these matters. He presented as a secretive rather than a withdrawn child, but nobody knew how he really felt.

Before meeting him I learned that Peter had one very absorbing interest — football. I arranged to see the whole family at my first meeting with Peter. There were several other children, including another foster child, in this family. I did not wish to arrive and go off immediately into another room with the 'ill' member, Peter, for some mysterious session. So I was in fact greeted by all six children, both foster parents, two dogs and a rabbit. I arrived with a whole lot of little party puzzles, games and quizzes. All the children joined in the fun but I engineered it so that I finished up being shown by Peter how the football game was played and what the rules were.

Peter, who was a child of normal intelligence, sorted out the rules and

FIG. 2

'Getting to Know You' boards (Familymakers' Homefinding Unit)

'explained' most of them to me. The rest we sorted out together. Before making this first visit I had also found out something about the football team I knew Peter 'followed'. You will see from this that a fair amount of work and planning went into even the first introduction meeting between me and Peter. Afterwards I never had any difficulty in getting on with him. Some very difficult areas of discussion lay ahead and it was as well to build on good foundations. Note, again, that I let Peter *contribute* by explaining the rules of the game to me. Another thing to notice is that I deliberately planned the scenario of my playing first with the children as a group.

I find it does help to set the stage, to ensure the situation is comfortable or that the scenario is likely to be suitable for the first meeting. Sometimes I have arranged to take the child out to the local shops so as to purchase a few little articles which I intended to use in my direct work. I may plan to call at a newsagents to get a little exercise book for use in writing the child's story, or getting him to write it. Or perhaps we'd go and buy a 'scrap book' as they are useful for making Life Story Books.

You may find it very helpful to do a bit of shopping or to arrange some other informal activity. It gives child and adult a chance to chat easily. It turns the first meeting into something other than an interview. This sort of activity-situation also helps you to learn about one another quite quickly. You may come to see at first hand just what a clever manipulator the child can be as he skilfully attempts to persuade you to purchase half the goods in the shop. Hopefully, it is also an opportunity for the child to learn that you are not a 'push-over'.

For the person coming in, so to speak, to work with the child it is probably best to use the first meeting just to get to know one another, although you still need the right situation or a third object activity even to do that well. I remember once, before I'd had much experience, going to visit a young girl in a children's home run by a religious order. I was *put* into a sort of committee room and sat at one end of a vast table. After what seemed ages the young lass, aged about fourteen, was brought into the presence and was made to stand at the opposite end of the table. The scenario was not helpful.

I want to encourage my readers to *invent* special third objects and maybe adapt them to new children, and also to pass the ideas on to other workers. At some early stage in a direct work programme you can make use of any 'game' or other activity you have designed. Figure 2 shows two boards for a game called *Getting to Know You* which has been used successfully by the *Familymakers* Homefinding Unit (1983). The worker and child each have a board. Each player draws, in the different squares, important people or things in their lives. Then they 'play' on their partner's board. They use dice and markers. When the marker lands on a square (which it does whenever one shakes the dice) then, as the rules say, ''You can either ask the other player specific questions about the drawing or ask the other player to talk in general about the drawing''. *Familymakers* have found this game helpful in getting children to express feelings about people and events in their lives. Remember, however, that not every child is able to play that particular game straight off. Your own sensitivity and understanding must be used here.

Don't overlook the more conventional activities such as painting pictures, or crayoning, or trying out what a toy telephone sounds like. And if you haven't got a toy telephone or a walkie-talkie, and the child is old enough, try making a 'telephone' with a couple of old cans and length of stout string. You must have heard of this old pastime. You pierce the bottom of each tin can, pass the string through from the outside, tie a big knot which won't slip through the hole, pull the 'line' tight with a can at each end. Then one person listens whilst the other talks. Most of all, use your imagination.

FOCUSSING ON LIFE TRAIL;

I now come to an area of work which is essential and central to the task of preparing children for long-term placement, or indeed, helping them to sort out their own identity. I shall describe a number of methods or 'games' used to help the child to establish in his mind as accurate as possible a picture of his life history. I have already mentioned the reasons for doing this direct work. However, it is worth while reiterating that although in this section I am intending to show the reader how these tools can be used to help the child obtain a clearer picture of his life history, the games and devices will, at the same time, usually be registering other aspects and helping the child and worker to learn about feelings and wishes as well as history.

It is worthwhile saying more about this *self-identity* concept. Triseliotis (1983) states:

> Concepts such as identity, security, sense of belonging are elusive and difficult to define or measure.

But when discussing his study, which contrasted a sample of people who grew up adopted, against a sample of people who grew up in long-term fostering, he identifies three 'areas' which appear to make a big contribution to 'identity building'. They are:

(i). A childhood experience of feeling wanted and loved within a secure environment.

(ii). Knowledge about one's background and personal history; and,

(iii). The experience of being perceived by others as a worthwhile person.

Each of these areas, and others, may be explored in ways helpful to the child by using the forms of communication described here provided the adult involved is sensitive to the child's signals, tactful, skilful and patient.

Life flow charts:

This is a method which I've found helpful in giving children a quick, panoramic view of their lives. I explained in Chapter One how I came to use this idea when working with Jamie. The idea is quite simple but usually very effective, and the variations on the main theme are many. Essentially the flow chart is a series of boxes representing different periods and places linked together in a line to represent time (Figure 3).

The way the flow chart is used will depend very much on the age and intelligence of the child and other factors such as how much, in the worker's estimation, the child already knows. Often it is helpful if a certain amount of preparation on the flow chart has already gone on before the child starts to use it. For example, the worker may have drawn out a series of six boxes representing six fairly distinct periods in the child's life. Each period may represent a different 'placement' in the child's life. The boxes could be left quite empty or they could have the names of the previous caregivers already written in, but in any case they would have the age of the child or an age bracket written above the box in this way:

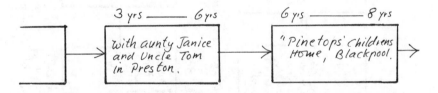

Sometimes the child I am helping has a clear memory picture of events and people of the last two or three years, or she feels she has, but beyond that is a kind of void so I may suggest that she starts with where she is now and then works backwards. We may then be discussing, early in the use of the flow chart, the reason why she came to the present caregivers who could be the staff of a Children's Home. A little later we would be talking about the place she lived at just before that last move and the people she lived with, and the reasons for the last move. Sometimes we have started with the 'being born' bit first, even if the bit in the middle is hazy. Most children want to know where they were born, how much they weighed and who their parents were, and such is the curiosity that it often makes the communication easier.

Of course I don't stick to dry old boxes. This is where our imagination has to come in. There are all sorts of attractive games that can be played on the flow chart theme. I may, for example, have a series of interesting shapes and give them different colours, like this:-

FIG. 3

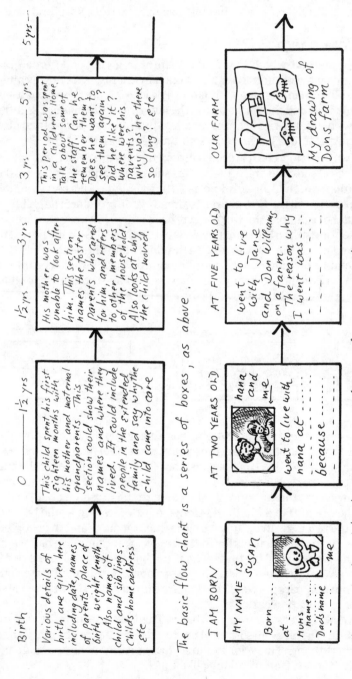

The basic flow chart is a series of boxes, as above.

Many children like to use gummed 'Joycraft' squares which come in various colours, and then they can stick drawings or photographs on these squares.

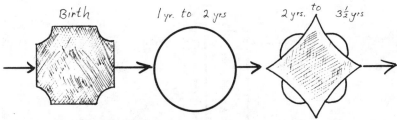

Whenever possible the child is encouraged to colour the shapes in (watercolour or powder paints are best if you wish to write inside the shapes afterwards), and of course some children may like to choose the shapes or even to draw them in but this needs some control as they tend either to draw minute shapes which cannot be used for writing in or sticking small or cut down photographs in, or they go to the other extreme and produce shapes so big that you'd need a motorway to roll the flow charts out. However, it is quite fun for younger children when they stick rolls together in order to get all their life on and then we have to stretch it out across the floor to read it or work on it, so don't cramp their style just because you want a nice neat little Life Flow Chart.

Another method is to use the large coloured, gummed squares of paper. These are about 15cm x 15cm (approx 6'' x 6'') and the ones I have used were known as 'Jollycraft' gummed paper squares. Or if the worker or the child want to be artistically ambitious they can design a little railway train with a line of waggons or carriages, finishing up 'where we are now' with the engine. (Figure 4).

It is important for us to remember that the separate stages, be they repesented by boxes or houses or anything else, are to be used to help the child and the worker to learn. Things must be written or drawn inside the boxes. These may be statements, drawings, observations, or even temporarily unanswered questions. Sometimes these may be pencilled in so that later information may be inserted and the question rubbed out. Also, if the boxes or the railway trucks or whatever become full, do not worry about writing things outside them with lines or arrows going towards the boxes:

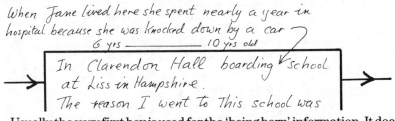

Usually the very first box is used for the 'being born' information. It does not need to have all the facts appertaining to the child's birth added immediately. Sometimes the worker will know that certain information

FIG. 4

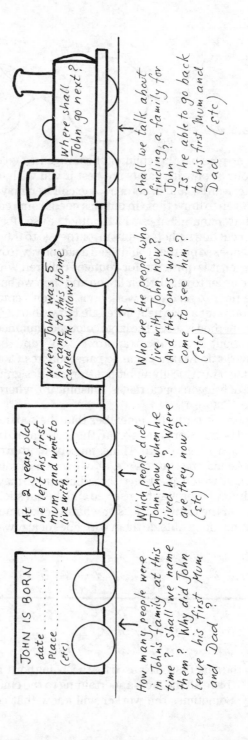

Flow chart for young child.

which could be disturbing has never been given to the child. A professional sensitivity is very important in the use of these devices and it may be far better to leave things out, at least to begin with, and to wait until either an appropriate question comes from the child, or the worker becomes aware that it is really necessary for the child to receive that particular information. For example, many children do not know who their natural father is. It would be an insensitive use of the flow chart method (particularly dangerous in a printed pack form) if the worker went about completing the first box as if it were some sort of official form or income tax return, or indeed supplying the child with all the facts simply because the flow chart had been used in this way with other children. This should be remembered when considering the sort of information going into the first or 'being born' box.

Another decision that should be taken in regard to all the instruments we are discussing is the decision as to whether they are to be used both for private work and for the child to show to other people, or whether they are only for private work, something which the child and the worker use in private to enable both to learn things which are confidential. These Flow Charts, Life Story Books, and other things will then remain confidential unless either the child wishes to discuss them with or show them to someone else, or he gives permission for them to be shown to others. In practice the Life Story Book tends to be produced with a wider circulation in view, and I have found that some children will bring it out in order to let visitors or comparative strangers see it. Other children, even when 'skeletons in the cupboard' have been left out, seem to want to keep it hidden and do not use it as a photograph album might be used.

I have tended to use the flow chart more as a working tool which was not for general publication. In this way things could be written down or shown in drawings which the child did not wish to go into a Life Story Book intended to be read by others (even rather special others). Because, don't forget, when you reach a certain box you may get into an intense area concerned with how the child feels now about his or her parents and other members of the family. Don't forget, you will be using the flow chart for *feelings* as well as for history. And it is important, if the child wants to use it just for private work, that you let him or her know that no-one else sees this chart.

With the flow chart, as with the other communicating methods, it is also important not to rush its use. I have sometimes had flow charts on the go for several months. Where the child's placement history has been complicated and complex, perhaps with many moves, the use of the Life Flow Chart often helps to get things straight and to disentangle muddled ideas before going on to the Life Story Book.

The flow chart principle is successfully incorporated into other attractive devices, some of which may be used for the same purpose. Figure 6

FIG. 5

'Being Born' box of a flow chart

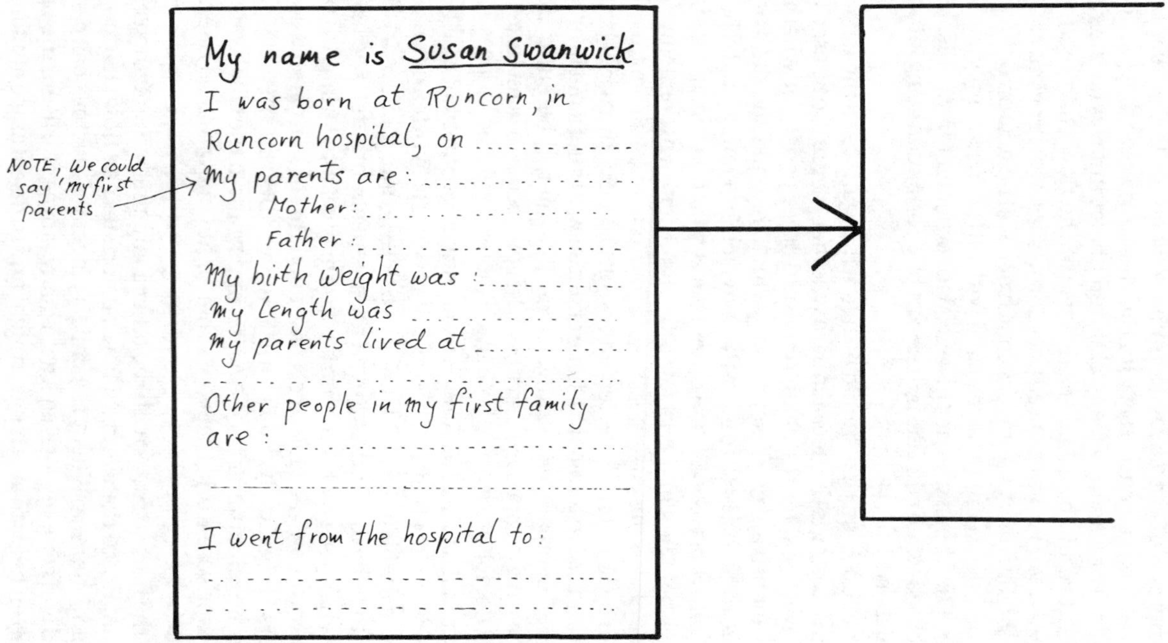

My name is <u>Susan Swanwick</u>

I was born at Runcorn, in
Runcorn hospital, on ....
my parents are:
    Mother: ....
    Father: ....
My birth weight was : ....
my length was ....
my parents lived at ....

Other people in my first family
are : ....

I went from the hospital to: ......
....
....

NOTE, we could
say, my first
parents

These are examples of details which might be found in a 'Being Born' box shows the idea used in a three dimensional manner, using the idea of a bus journey with a starting point, this being the bus station (the hospital in real life where the child was born) and showing a number of 'stops' with a building at each of the stops. A space is left either on or near the building for the child or worker to write in. Each of the 'stops' represents a stage or an actual placement in the child's life, so that child and worker decide what place each 'stop' represents. What were the names of the important people in the child's life at that 'stop'? How did the child feel at that 'stop'? Why had he to move to another 'stop'? — and so on. It is possible to make the model either painted flat on a large piece of paper or, if one wants to be more 'ambitious' or make use of model making as part of the therapy or 'third object', to actually construct cardboard buildings and stand them along the route. In either example a real toy bus or car may be used.

The main advantage of the flow chart idea is that it helps the child to retain or actually construct a picture of past events and to see where her roots lie. It helps her to trace her own history. Whilst this is happening other learning may be taking place, both in child and worker. At one point along the flow chart we may touch on matters which throw up feelings of anger, or grief, or indignation. Elsewhere in this book we discuss the need to work with these feelings and to help the child to express them and to resolve them.

Since we are discussing the use of the flow chart in direct work with children it is worthwhile mentioning the value of this method as a tool for the worker's use before the commencement of any work with the child. John Fitzgerald (1983) prints a blank flow chart in his booklet and states that this may be photocopied without applying for permission and used in children's files. This way of using flow charts as a guide to the workers and the care agency, and as a preparation exercise before undertaking direct work with a child concentrates one in a way other methods do not, particularly if dates and names are put in. The method even shows up discrepancies on the files and makes one search for missing information. It also gives the teams who are planning for the children an overall view of what has happened so far in the lives of the children. Naturally, flow charts used in this way will not be the colourful (or messy!) things the children may be using. They will tend to be straightforward linked-up boxes.

Fitzgerald, in the work on disruption (fostering or adoption breakdown) referred to above, reports on the remarks made by the chairperson at the disruption meeting regarding 'Michael' (whose case is set out in full):

'He said that at many disruption meetings held by BAAF where the family was present, they realised as the story unfolded that this was not the same as the history of the child which they had received. The question of how material is presented to families so that they can understand what it means to be a child in care was also critical. The use of flow

FIG. 6

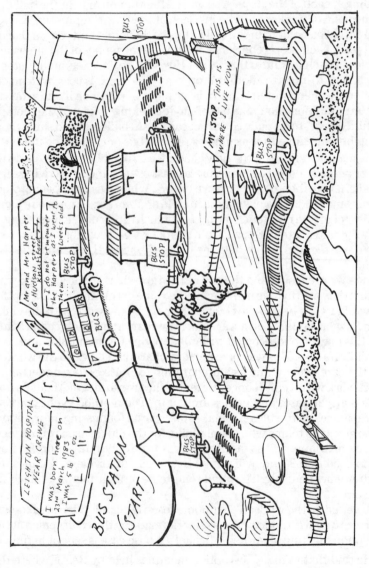

Bus journey flow chart

<u>charts</u>, such as the one reproduced here for Michael, and other visual material, <u>was recommended as one possibility!</u> (My underlining). (BAAF — British Agencies for Adoption and Fostering).

Obviously workers will come up with all sorts of imaginative variations on the flow chart principle. The elongated jigsaw with spaces underneath the jigsaw pieces is another variation. This has also come into our use from being first tried at the Catholic *Familymakers* Homefinding Unit:

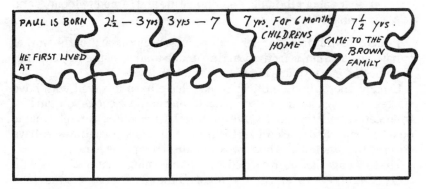

Life Story Books.

These have been in use for several years now in child care circles, and in fact there is a danger that sometimes they may now be prescribed and used without imagination when some agency decrees that all its childlren should have their Life Story Book 'done' in the same way as all children get registered at birth or immunised a bit later on.

I want to talk about them as instruments or third objects which can be of the utmost help when used sensitively, and even selectively. I am not against children making up albums and sticking in photos and other memorabilia just for the fun of it. That's fine, but we must not imagine that this exhausts the use of the Life Story Book.

In fact, so adaptable is this method of working with children that it is possible, if you know what you are doing, to cover all the categories I have listed; Starters, Focussing On Life Trail, Discussion Directing, the lot. The way it is used will depend very much on the skill and enthusiasm of the person working with the child.

Before going on to describe in greater detail my own use of Life Story Books, I feel another word of warning is appropriate. Life Story Books, as I have said, together with flow charts and some other techniques are sometimes being used before the child is ready to benefit from these methods. This applies particularly to very disturbed and perhaps withdrawn children. Some very damaged and emotionally deprived children will need help, in the first place, which takes the form of free- or non-focussed play. They may need regression play and nurture enrichment experiences, as described in Chapter Four of this book, before moving on to the more focussed or directed activities I am describing here. Do not force the pace with highly disturbed children.

The Life Story Book as I have used it seems to have three valuable aims:

1. To give the child an account of his/her beginnings and history.
2. To act as a third object.
3. To be used as a therapeutic tool enabling child and worker to learn about the child's emotional life and to modify feelings and behaviour.

To meet this third set of aims it will of course be necessary for the worker to have imagination, sensitivity and an understanding of the way children develop and can be damaged or hurt emotionally.

Usually, then, the Life Story Books I have been involved with have started off as just an empty 'scrap book', one of those books you can buy from stationers or toy shops. Quite often we have coloured the child's name on white paper and stuck this on the front of the book. Sometimes we have covered the whole scrap book with coloured wrapping paper.

The first page has often carried an announcement that this is the 'Life Story Book of............' and then a photograph and/or the name of the child. Somewhere at the beginning we have put in details of the child's birth, and then the story has proceeded from there.

Some of the books have been colourful, some have been neat, some have been untidy. Some have looked brand new at the end of the day, others have looked dog-eared. Some have all sorts of bits and pieces in them; photographs, birthday cards, drawings, letters, or large envelopes serving as pockets for holding anything from dried leaves to a "bit of my mum's hair". Others have just been written straight through as a story. Some were actually written by the child, others were written out by the adult working with the child. So you see there is plenty of scope.

I've already introduced Jamie in Chapter One. What was it like doing a life story book with him? Remember, I'd already mapped out his life with him when we used the flow chart. His flow chart was still in use when we started his Life Story Book so many of the details, especially details about his birth, how much he weighed, where he was born, were already there for us to use. But I had to do some other work:

Jamie: "What does Walton hospital look like?"
Me: "Didn't you go and see it when you lived in Liverpool?"
Jamie: "I can't remember. I'd like to see it".
Me: "O.K., maybe I could take you over there. Do you want to put a cover on this book before we start, or will you just have your name on the front?"
Jamie: "I know, let's stick some of that red paper on first. I'll cut it out. Where are the scissors?"

Jamie proceeded to cut out.

Jamie: (while sticking) "When can I go and see Walton Hospital?"
Me: "Will you like seeing it?"
Jamie: "Yes......... this won't stick............ that's got it. Yes, I think I'll like it".
Me: "Why? Why do you think it's nice seeing Walton Hospital?"

Now he'd started to crayon.

Jamie: "The other kids at school talk about where they were born..... What shall we put on the first page?"
Me: "How about starting with a photograph of you and then writing 'This is the Life Story of Jamie?'"
Jamie: "No......... that sounds stupid".
Me: "What then?"
Jamie: "I know, we'll take a photograph of Walton Hospital and put that in first".

And so the structuring, and conversing, and planning would go on. Sometimes we'd come to a special point. For example, when referring to a photograph about some earlier foster parents who had intended to take Jamie permanently:

Me: "This is a picture of you taken when you were on holiday with Uncle Wilf and Auntie Rose........ can you remember that holiday?"
Jamie: "We don't need that one in........ I know, I'll cut them off and just put me in......... where are the scissors?"
Me: "But if you do that your book won't really tell us about all the people you met, will it?"
Jamie: (ignoring me) "I'll just cut along here........"
Me: "Why not put them in too?"
Jamie: "I can't get these photo-corners to fit on now I've cut me off".
Me: "When did you have that holiday? You must be about three there, would you say?"
Jamie: "Yes, nearly three........ I remember that tricycle......... Will you write something in there, while I find another picture....... no, a post card".
Me: (After writing in a short description). "So that picture was taken just before you went to live somewhere else?"
Jamie: (busy) "Yep".

There followed a short silence while we both worked on the book. Then I said:

"Can you remember why you went away from Auntie Rose and Uncle Wilf?"

Jamie:	"You know".
Me:	"But you and I may not have the same story........ what is the book going to say?"
Jamie:	"D'you think we've done enough book now?"
Me:	"I'll tell you what, we'll just decide what to say about your leaving Auntie Rose and Uncle Wilf then we'll play badminton in the garden".
Jamie:	"Well I don't really want to say why I moved because I don't like to........ (here he worked away with a paint brush and felt pens). Auntie Rose never did like kids who wet the beds......... but we'll not put that in".
Me:	"No, of course we won't......... but is that what you were told? Did someone say you left because you wet the bed?"
Jamie:	"Yep........ I still do, well I'm not *so* bad now".

There then followed a great disclosure by me. You see I knew from other sources that his enuresis was not the reason for his having to move from the Stanards. We cannot go into the real reasons now.

The session described above was very fruitful. It emerged, but until then no-one, not even Jamie, had said so, that this child not only experienced a cut-off point by a set of caregivers but had associated that in his mind with bed-wetting. In other words, not only was he rejected (from his point of view), but he was rejected because of something *nasty* about himself. For him to carry such beliefs into the next family would quite likely have caused disruptive behaviour. Maybe he would have *had* to wet the bed in order to test-out the new parents. But we can also see how the child's life experience can affect his self-image.

The Walton hospital discussion, apart from the value of the experience of going back and standing outside (and inside) the place where he was born, was also important from a self-identity standpoint. Having gone back and stood there Jamie would be able to talk with confidence as 'the other kids at school did'.

When I am using Life Story Books or flow charts or almost any other third object, I am always wanting to create opportunities to learn about the child's ideas and feelings, and also of course I want to convey new ideas to the child. That is why, when I use the Life Story Book, I am using it as something much more productive than an ordinary album, valuable though an album may be.

Jamie and I had discussed in some detail his feelings towards his natural mother and his sisters and stepfather. These discussions had taken place while working on the flow chart. However, all these people were discussed again as we stuck photographs, letters and birthday cards into the Life Story Book:

Jamie:	"See there, Mum's got her arm round Susan again....... that's how she is with our Susan".

Me:	"Did she put her arm round you?"
Jamie:	"Sometimes......... not as much though".
Me:	"How about Sandra?"
Jamie:	"She used to get me into trouble........I always got the belt because of her.........can I paint a picture now?"
Me:	"Yes, you just finish off that page then I'll get the painting things".

A few minutes later:

Jamie:	"What shall I paint?"
Me:	:"Well, do you still feel angry about your mum or your sisters?"
Jamie:	"Yes........It was my mum's fault too.......I used to get the blame because she told my dad".
Me:	"Did you ever draw a picture, or paint one for your mum?"
Jamie:	"No.........she only laughed at them".
Me:	"Did she say anything else about them?"
Jamie:	"'Rubbish', she said.........I know, I'll draw our dad's belt with studs all over it".

He starts to paint something resembling a snake extending all over the large sheet of paper.

Jamie:	"And here's our mum, standing shouting at me".
Me:	"Can you think of some nice things about your mum?"
Jamie:	(after a pause)........"Well, I *sort of* liked her, that's why I kept going home.........she didn't like me much........well, if she didn't have Sandra and Susan she would 'ave".

By this time Jamie was able to accept that it 'would not work out' if he went home. You have to be careful when doing direct work like this. You must work within the *actual possibilities* so far as planning is concerned. Jamie had had seventeen moves by the time he was eight. He had been hospitalised from home with 'at risk' symptoms on at least two occasions. The time had come, if it was not already too late, to find some other form of permanent care for him. So in a way his choice was limited. He would not be placed at home with his natural mother. He might, however, have shown me that he was not ready for fostering.

But Jamie was now agreeing, and I felt sure we were right, that going back home would not work out. The book and the flow chart had both been used to help him to talk and to learn. They had also helped me in the same way.

I don't think I would say that there was no attachment at all by Jamie to his natural mother, or no bonding on her part. But there is a state known as *'insecure attachment'.* The worker needs to ascertain, as far as possible, not only the degree of attachment but the quality of the child's attachment to the adult caregiver. This is an area of study too extensive to be covered in this book (see Further Reading list). I was interested in the *quality* of Jamie's attachment to his natural mother and siblings.

You will remember that Wendy ultimately returned to live with her own mother. There has been controversy over the policy of placing children permanently in families other than their natural families. As is usual with such controversies, this has tended to produce polarisation with some people failing to accept the possibility of damage, if not total destruction, to some children by leaving them at home, whilst their opposites have forgotten the importance of supportive work which could have maintained children within their own families. We need to develop and maintain our skills in discovering what is best for *particular* children and in meeting those needs. Wendy gave me plenty of signals as I worked with her. Here are a few snippets from conversations we had when working on her Life Story Book:

Me:	"You've got a nice little pile of letters here, do you want to put those in?"
Wendy:	"Let's read them again first......I've got three from you...... and six, no seven, from Nana and Grandad".

She straightens out the letters and then addresses me by using an intonation I've come to associate with her when introducing what to her is an important area for discussion, perhaps something causing anxiety, or some request she wants to make:

Wendy:	"Ke-en?"
Me:	"Yes?"
Wendy:	"I haven't got any letters from Bob Walters" (her stepfather).
Me:	"No".
Wendy:	"I wish I had".

Here tears begin to show in the corner of her eyes. A pause follows while I collect the odd birthday card and letter together. Wendy has suddenly 'frozen' and is staring at the floor.

Me:	"Do you want to talk about Bob?......shall we see if you have any photographs of him?"
Wendy:	"It's Sandra Griffiths' fault......I hate her!"

Sandra Griffiths is the social worker who was involved earlier and had to receive Wendy into care when the family broke up.

Me:	(after a pause) "Why do you hate her?"
Wendy:	"She's told Bob not to write to me......she......"

Here Wendy burst into tears. At this point the temptation was to put the book away for a bit and turn to something else because the session seemed to be too painful, for me as well as Wendy. But it was important, if we could, to follow some of this through because here was a vital mental scenario of Wendy's which could be causing problems at the moment and would cause more problems in the future. Wendy was clearly directing anger at the social worker. But how much attachment existed towards Bob the stepfather?

Me: "How about you drawing a picture for Bob Walters?"
Wendy: (her eyes now dry again) "I could make him a calendar"
Me: "That's a good idea, let's find some pretty calendar things".

In the middle of the calendar making when Wendy seemed settled again, I popped a question which led on to her revealing another anxiety. She seemed to feel Bob Walters had rejected her:

Me: "Did you call Bob Walters 'Dad'?"
Wendy: "Yes".
Me: "You're making a beautiful calendar......is Bob *special?*"
Wendy: (while cutting out)"......he used to love me".
Me: "Doesn't he still love you?"

Wendy shook her head. Whatever she had said and felt concerning the social worker she also felt that Bob himself had withdrawn his love.

I cannot extend these extracts from that particular session with Wendy but the reader will see that a number of very important factors emerged and these needed to be picked up and involved in the work with the child, though not necessarily just at that time.

In point of fact, Bob Walters was fond of Wendy but he had got himself into an arrangement wherein he was not permitted to continue with any kind of relationship with her. The woman he had set up in partnership with accepted his own children but would not have anything to do with Wendy or anyone else associated with Bob's previous marriage.

So even from these brief exchanges we see that Wendy was holding wrong ideas about people and their motives. These would affect her feelings and therefore her behaviour. Bob Walters was not in fact rejecting her (later I did get him to write to her). But Wendy was also going to need help in accepting the loss of this attachment figure in her life. And then there was her anger directed against the social worker who in fact did not prevent Bob from writing to Wendy. Perhaps we could accept that anger for the time being, but on the other hand Wendy would do better if she could ultimately understand the real motives of people who had to receive her into care.

Here is another extract which concerned Wendy's feelings towards her mother and towards other possible caregivers. The discussions toook place after she had left the Ormrods:

Wendy: "We need a picture of this children's home".

Me:	"Yes......tell you what, I'll bring my camera next week and take one of you in the garden......but anyway you've got to put these pictures in yet haven't you?" (These were photographs taken at the Ormrods).
Wendy:	"I don't think I'll have those in".
Me:	"Why not......your book will have a piece missing from it if you leave them out".
Wendy:	"I only want my family......and my mum".
Me:	"Suppose you go to a new family......I mean your mum's said she can't have you".
Wendy:	"Have you seen her?"
Me:	"No......that was a long time ago. But I'm still trying to find her for you".
Wendy:	"Let's not do any more..... can we play that game where I'm captured, I'm a princess, and you rescue me?"

This was a piece of role-play done to music played on a tape recorder or record player.

Me:	"Yes, in a minute, just colour that piece in. So, suppose you do go to another family?"
Wendy:	"I don't want to......I never want to".

Perhaps, if things had been different, this matter would have been raised again maybe several months later, by me. But at this time the conversation went on.

Wendy:	"Anyway, my grandad's coming for me on Saturday......he won't let me go......Nan says I look like my mum".
Me:	"That's nice".
Wendy:	(Packing the Life Story Book away) "I'll put a picture of me and my mum on the front......then when you find her she can see it".

I did find her, and Wendy did return to her care. But a lot of preparation went into her return home and the family needed a lot of support afterwards when they were reunited.

I hope these extracts, Jamie's and Wendy's, have in some small way reflected the three aims referred to earlier, that is to say (1) providing a life history), (2) providing a third object, and (3) as a therapy tool concerning the child's feelings and behaviour, and shown the reader the way in which the Life Story Book is used by me.

I think that Jamie and Wendy did have rather different needs. They were both in varying degrees 'mixed up', but Jamie could not have been helped by being returned to his natural mother's care. Wendy could be, and was, helped by being reunited with her mother.

Life Story Books — practical details.

Usually I have used 'scrap books' (Figure 7) as Life Story Books. But even here one has to be rather sensitive to the child's feelings. Many scrap books look 'babyish' with all sorts of pretty little coloured motifs embellishing the front cover. Some older children would see this as insulting their youth. The reader will note that in Figure 7 Clare Jones, aged eight, has coloured in her name, etc. at the top but we've left all the little motifs showing at the bottom, whereas Jonathan Williams, aged fifteen and quite artistic, started with a white cover and did some nice lettering.

There are many ways of structuring the Life Stories and many ways of presenting them. There are also many ways of actually working on them. The adult will need to decide whether, as in the case of a very young or handicapped child, she is going to write down what the child says or whether the child will do all the handwriting. Some children do tire quickly. An alternative is to mix it, so the child may write short statements such as 'This is a picture of my Auntie Doris' whilst the adult writes the longer statements. But the child must know what is to be written: 'Shall we say "This is William when he went to camp with the Cubs. He is holding the big fish he caught"?'

Sometimes the life stories are written in a traditional story manner and done by the adult *with* the child. This may be necessary as a run-through before doing another type of work. We have often used match-stick figure drawings to represent people in the child's life. The story may actually start off with 'Once upon a time......' (Figure 8).

The stories are usually structured so that the beginning pages say something about the child's birth parents. It is necessary to pitch this opening part very much at the child's level of understanding and behaviour. It doesn't matter so much about the *age* of the child, it is his ability to understand that dictates the style of the story. So the first page, after the heading, might start off 'There lived a very nice young lady who had long dark brown hair which reached down to her shoulders. She was called Janet Downing......' This is the start of a description of the child's natural mother. On the other hand, with many children the books are not as descriptive to begin with and they tend to start with matter-of-fact details about the child's birth, the parents' names, etc., and even 'family trees'. Figure 9 shows an open book which has this kind of treatment and includes a photograph of the hospital in which the child was born.

Usually, for the purpose of preparation, the Life Story Book is used to help the child develop a healthy self-image and self-identity. This means that while the material, drawings, post-cards, made-up poems, letters received, photographs, etc., are going into the book in chronological order we are also using the material for 'talk' with the child: 'Do you sometimes think about your first daddy?' Such a question *may* come from the adult

FIG. 7

Life Story Books

FIG. 8

Story with match-stick people

FIG. 9

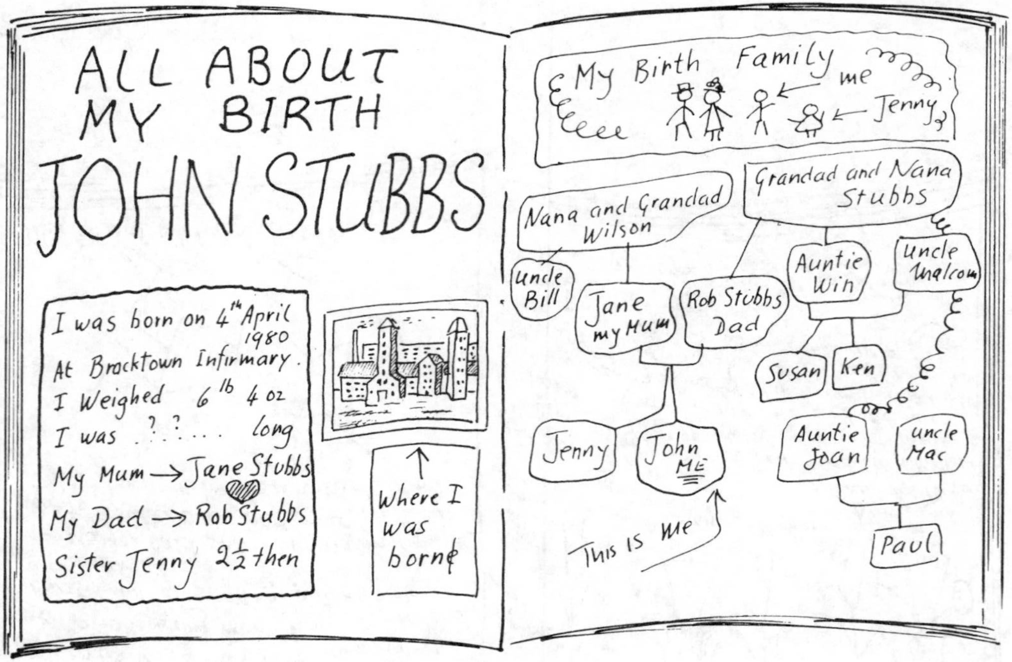

ALL ABOUT
MY BIRTH
JOHN STUBBS

I was born on 4th April 1980.
At Brocktown Infirmary.
I weighed 6 lb 4 oz
I was ? ? .... long
My Mum → Jane Stubbs
My Dad → Rob Stubbs
Sister Jenny 2½ thrn

Where I was born↑

My Birth Family
me ← Jenny

Grandad and Nana Stubbs

Nana and Grandad Wilson

Uncle Bill

Jane my Mum

Rob Stubbs Dad

Auntie Win

Susan

Ken

Uncle Ingloux

Auntie Joan

Uncle Mac

Paul

Jenny

John Me

This is me

Life Story Book : Starting page

FIG. 10

FIG. 11

as a picture of the child's father is stuck in. Or the child may say "Why did my first mummy go away?"

Extraordinary things occur in connection with Life Story Books. One child known to me 'discovered' his only near relatives during the writing of the story. The relatives were his paternal grandparents. Their discovery came about because the staff of the Children's Home set about searching for early photographs and other mementos for the child, then aged about thirteen. For several years he had been in care, abandoned by both natural parents, and with all other relatives seemingly 'lost'. (Figure 10).

Sometimes, as the Life Story develops, special pages can be devoted to special events such as a move to a new family, or even 'My tenth birthday' as in Figure 11.

Another helpful idea I have used is to include pages which say something about the child now. These pages can have statements, cuttings, drawings and paintings to show things like: 'My favourite song is......', 'I like to.....'etc. Another idea is to write about memories: 'My dad liked.....', 'In our home there was......'

I have occasionally helped a child to combine the Life Story Book idea with the flow chart idea by incorporating a mini flow chart in the Life Story Book. It may be that the child has had a special holiday or she remembers the six months spent in a children's home, and this separate period can be illustrated by way of a pull-out flow chart. The flow chart is attached to the book by some adhesive. (See Figure 12).

Some children have an intense need to express certain inner anxieties in the form of drawing or painting. They often have a recurring theme. One child, Steven, who had witnessed violence to the person in the form of his mother's suicide spent several months drawing the sort of violence-picture shown in Figure 13.

Children value what we may see as scribbles. Life Story Books do not have to contain neat drawings. Four-year-olds are happy to describe their contributions according to their own insight imagination. Figure 14 gives some examples.

The expression of emotional experience or 'feelings' in art form does seem to be beneficial to many children and young people. However, not all children will wish to incorporate these drawings or poems or 'feeling stories' into their books. It will depend very much on how public they wish to make their Life Story Book. It is a good idea to fix some items in by using photograph corners, or paper fasteners, or by simply putting a little dab of past on each corner. Then, after the book has been used in a special therapeutic way, some things may be removed and others substituted. In Figures 15 a/b we do show some feeling drawings made by a seventeen year old girl, Dionne. Notice the frightening comparison of the soft, gentle flower surrounded by the dangerous tooth-lined jaws. Another of her feeling pictures shows two plants. The one on the right is a sort of ivy against

FIG. 12

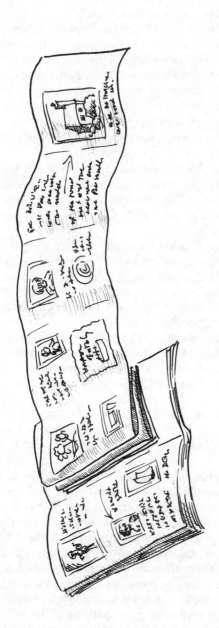

A mini pull-out flow chart.

FIG. 13

A violence-picture. One of dozens drawn by a child who witnessed the suicide of his mother by throat slashing.

FIG. 14

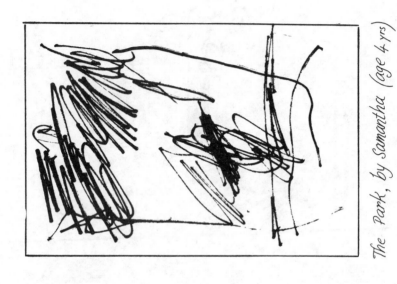

The Park, by Samantha (age 4 yrs)

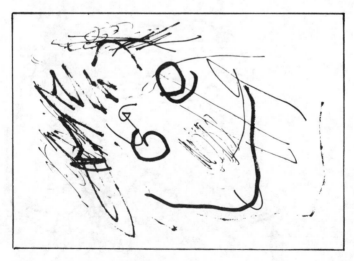

Samantha's 'First Mummy'

A wild feeling

By Dionne

FIG. 15b

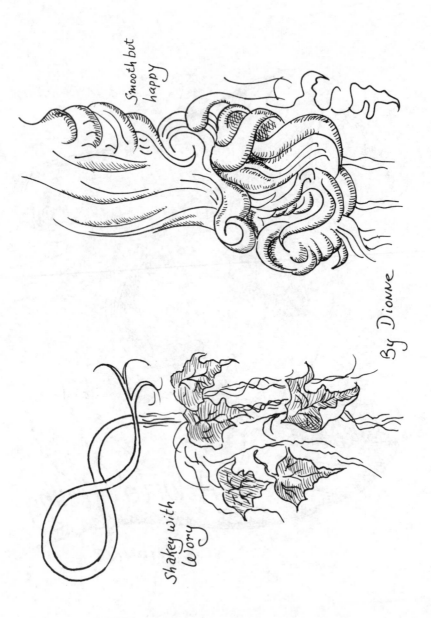

Smooth but happy

Shakey with Wory

By Dionne

which she has written 'shakey with worry'. The left-hand plant is more integrated and smooth. Against this she's written 'smooth but happy'. The picture itself is called 'A day of fun, good news, but nervous'.

As with other methods used during preparation the adult must pick up quickly any indications that the child is tiring or not able to cope with a particular avenue of enquiry at that juncture. Sometimes half an hour or longer is enjoyable, especially when the child becomes engrossed in making pictures. At another time even with the same child ten minutes may be long enough.

The person undertaking the direct work with the child should be able to recognise and handle the reactions produced. If they are not professionally trained and fairly experienced they must have supervision. In any case, it is always helpful for the adult involved to discuss this work with someone else since all of us tend to see events as we want to see them. The sort of reactions to expect, as well as enjoyment and excitement and relaxation, are anger, denial and regressive tendencies.

The Life Story Book should be read over from time to time with the child and items discussed, not simply written and then stored. A very helpful booklet on Life Story Book work has been written by Ryan and Walker (1985).

The danger I spoke of at the beginning of this section on Life Story Books lies in their unimaginative use where they become part of the routine. 'Has this child been done?' seems to be the attitude. We recently heard from a foster mother who had a well settled eight year old in her care. Suddenly, almost out of the blue, a social worker with whom neither the child nor the foster parents were acquainted 'phoned to say he'd be coming to 'do a Life Story Book with Jennifer' as one hadn't been done and, in their enthusiasm, the department had now decided to do this with all their children. The result was all but disastrous and it is not the way to use any of this material.

Sociogram Games.

This is another method of helping child and adult to learn about aspects of the Life Trail, but whereas the flow chart and the Life Story Book take an overall or panoramic view, this method enables us with the child to 'stop the motion picture' and examine one frame. It helps focus on a particular time anywhere along the Life Trail. Often it is used to look at the up-to-date situation, but it can just as readily be used to focus on a previous period in the child's life. We call this method the Sociogram method.

Sociograms have been used by social psychologists and other social scientists for some time now. Basically, a sociogram is a diagramatic method of showing the pattern of interpersonal relationships existing in any interaction group such as a family or a club or a local church. By analysing these relationships over a period of time it is possible to plot the interactional

FIG. 16

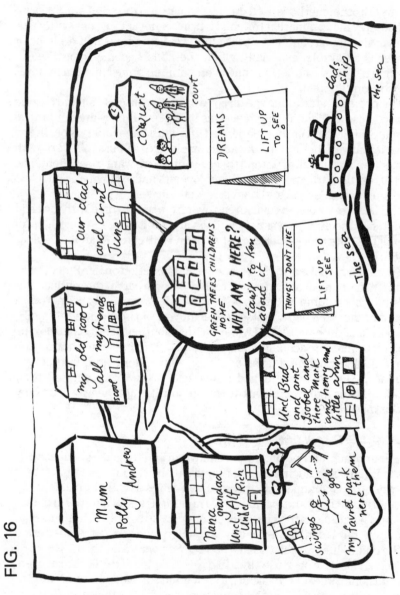

Sociogram or 'ecomap' drawn by an eight-year old

changes taking place within a group as well as viewing the relationships at any particular time. Although I have extended the application of the term somewhat, and although my diagrams (or the child's diagram) will not look so sophisticated as those made by the social psychologist, the main idea of plotting lines between various people to indicate positive or negative relationships, etc., is essentially the same. Other workers have used the sociogram idea in various ways to plot a picture of family relationships, etc. These usages have been given various names such as 'ecomap', 'genogram', and 'ecochart'.

Figure 16 shows a sort of mapped out plan, drawn by an eight year old as a result of encouragement from me. It is really a plan of how he felt various people fitted into his life and how they were linked to each other. This eight year old would not have been able to say, himself, that his drawing showed the interpersonal relationships of the extended family as he experienced them, but it did just that up to a point. The reader will appreciate also that I was learning about the way the child experienced these relationships.

In Figure 16 I suggested the child should draw houses for all the people he knew and wanted to think about so there would be a house for his Mum, and another for his 'Nana and Grandad' and so on. He started off by painting a circle in the middle of the paper with a drawing of 'Green Trees', the Children's Home he was living in, drawn inside the circle. The words written in block lettering 'WHY AM I HERE?' were put in by me as I wanted to have a discussion on that point with him.

Over a period of several weeks a lot emerged from the use of this sociogram drawing. Remember it was *fun* to be painting these houses. Remember, also, that it made it so much easier for the child to chatter about people and feelings as he was drawing and painting. And look at the little stuck-on lifting flaps. These were really extras and included one on dreams. The reader may feel that to bring dreams in is really spoiling the use of the sociogram as a method of ascertaining how the child and his extended family relate. But it is this kind of extemporising which is so valuable in direct work. It just so happened that when this particular sociogram drawing was in use, discussion on dreams and 'things I don't like' emerged so this was incorporated into the sociogram. I was not trying to create and use a scientific 'instrument', I was more concerned with communication between myself and the child, and with analysis of the material produced.

Here are a few more observations on the sociogram shown in Figure 16. Notice of course the two separate houses for this child's natural parents. Notice also the grouping of his extended family down the left hand side of the sociogram. There are a number of strong linking roads between these members, so that Uncle Bud, Aunt Isobel, Nana and Grandad, and Mum, Polly and Andrew all link up. This signifies either the real closeness of the extended family, or the child's experience of closeness, or a wish the child has to bring this about. The worker will need to discover which of these perceptions is valid and which is the actual message being transmitted. It is important, without *leading* the child, to find out which links are really strong (otherwise it could be that the weak lines were just due to the fact that the paint ran out at that point). It is necessary to chat about the sort of things the family members did together and what the child remembers about the closeness, the visiting, the outings, etc. Other information from the social worker involved with the family will also be available to the person undertaking direct work with the child. The picture can be made 'true' by going over certain lines, thickening them or painting them in a stronger colour if it is found, for example, that there are or were strong positive links actually existing. In this way the child begins to get a true picture.

In this sociogram the child has indicated what seems to be a happy memory about the park near to where Uncle Bud, Isobel and their children live. Notice the strong line going from the mother's home towards the home of his father, 'our Dad', and the person he calls Aunt June. This pathway stretches out towards Dad but is stopped abruptly. It becomes a cul-de-sac.

This child desperately wanted to unite his family. The stress between the natural parents and their ulimate separation, was probably a strong contributory factor in his coming before a court as being in need of care due to periodically running away from home, stealing, and showing other patterns of 'disturbed behaviour'. He puts in a drawing of the court building but he makes no link between this and himself or his family.

This child was also carrying a burden of anxiety about the possible permanent loss of his father to whom he was closely attached. This seems to be revealed in two ways: first, the only line going to the dreams is an offshoot from the path which leads from Dad down to the sea. One of the dreams (when you lifted the flap) was 'Another dream about saving our dad in a boat'. Second, there is the picture of the ship (the boat) in which his dad could get lost at sea.

Although a sociogram like the one I have been discussing may be used to obtain a picture of the child's perception of relationships at a given time in his or her history, the method may also be used for correcting the child's perception either about past, present or possible future situations. As a result of the time spent with the adult the child may construct another sociogram of the same period but depicting things as they really were. Of course, it would be possible for us to philosophise about how things 'really were', but we must maintain a fairly pragmatic approach here since some of the children do hold clearly muddled notions about some events in their lives. Events which we may easily be able to check on for more accurate information.

The final example I shall give of methods for focussing on the Life Trail is by making use of something which must be as old as history — the story. There are so many ways in which story telling may be used in direct work.

Story telling may be adapted to suit the needs of toddlers or teenagers. Story writing may be done by the adult entirely, or by adult and child, or by the child or young person on his or her own. I use the idea of the story to write or tell the story of the child in question. With young children this can start in the traditional story manner of 'Once upon a time there was a lday called Margaret......' Margaret would be the real name of the child's mother. Sometimes I gradually unfold the story with the help of the child. This is when we are writing the story together. It gives me an opportunity to discuss actual historical events and to correct the account. Another method I have used in order to ascertain what the child's perception is and how much this deviates from what I understand to be factual, is to say that I have written the story of Susan (the child) and as I read it will Susan please tell me if any parts are wrong. I then read out the story (factually correct as far as I know) but obtain the other 'correct' version from Susan. It is worth checking on the child's version of facts before attempting to draw up the final version. They can sometimes show us that our original 'true' story was not true!

Stories of course can be illustrated, and this gives further scope for the child to participate as well as giving the adult another area for research (through the media of drawing and painting). Teenagers often like to write their own stories of their lives. Some of these become romanticised or dramatised so that the correcting of them may be a matter for very careful consideration. There may in fact be parts which for the time being are better left uncorrected. Remember that in the direct work process the worker is learning, and through the medium of the story she may learn about the young person's need to project ideas about herself. These may be sort of emotional 'crutches' or, in psychoanalytic terminology, ego defences. When the child or young person has been given other strengths; when she has been given confidence, and has found acceptance by others she will usually be able to let go the 'crutches'. So we must be careful of our timing when correcting some of the views held.

Stories can usually be turned into plays. And I have sometimes used a set of small dolls (doll's house figures) and made one represent the child and others represent important people in the child's life. Then I have acted the story, making the dolls talk to each other whilst the child watched and listened. Some children like to take over, which is fine. But in order to go right through the life story I usually have to do some other scenes for the child, so we then take it in turns to act or watch. The story, of course, must be distinguished from the Life Story Book which is rather more of an album with the main story coming out in the photographs, drawings, letters, birth certificates, and other items.

I have produced a story written during work with a sibling group. This is found in Appendix 'A'. Dr. V. Fahlberg has some helpful things to say about Life Story Books. She also prints a life story written for a four year old by the worker concerned. (1981).

FIG. 17

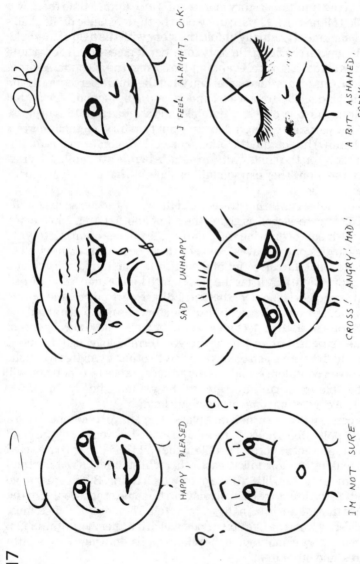

Face-cards used to help young children indicate their feelings

BARRIER-BREAKING:

When undertaking direct work with children, I found that it was necessary to invent little gadgets which proved helpful when dealing with those who felt shy in certain situations or who, even when they were not normally shy, found it difficult to communicate on matters which were very emotive. But it is verbal communication which often creates the barrier.

Verbal communication may be difficult simply because the child has a very limited vocabulary or it may be difficult to put into words complicated feelings. Sometimes it may be difficult for the child to open a discussion about something he or she really does want to talk about. Once they get into it they feel alright but it's hard to actually start talking about it.

Discussion Cards.

With young children who find it hard to say what they *feel* about certain things I have used one of the methods devised by Dr. Vera Fahlberg, the method of using face-cards. This is a set of cards which has the same face but showing different moods. One face is crying, the next card has it smiling, another has it looking very cross, and so on (Figure 17). I may say to the young child something like this: "When I show you this photograph how do you feel? Does it make you sad, like that face, or does it make you cross, like that one, or do you feel happy like that one? You point to the one that feels like you do".

The use of specially designed sets of cards can be very helpful. They may be used in a variety of ways to facilitate and to introduce discussion, and to introduce discussion, and also to guide the talk ('discussion' often sounds too formal a word). It may eventually be possible to purchase packs containing sets of such cards, but the sensitive worker should always be prepared to design cards especially to apply to the individual child in direct work. I shall refer to these cards again when we look at *Discussion-Directing*.

Another little gadget I have designed and used is the Slider (Figure 18). The fun principle here is that the child and the adult can move a little panel or slide window up and down a long card which has any desired number of items written on it. The person whose turn it is to select the item for 'talk' moves the slider over the item he wants to discuss, or which may indicate his feelings or wishes, etc. These sliders may be used to facilitate discussions generally, or to direct discussion, or to make it easier for a child to open a discussion about the way he or she feels. So we have called them subject-sliders, or feelings-sliders accordingly.

On Page 165 are three lists I used on sliders with a ten year old girl. The lists were given headings. Some of the items such as 'Mum being ill' were put in as it was felt from previous work with her that this was an area of

FIG. 18

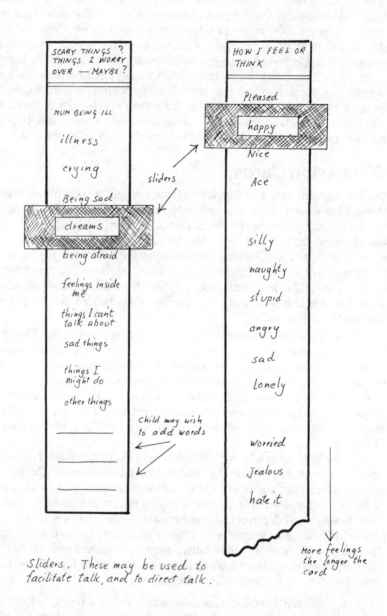

SCARY THINGS ?
THINGS I WORRY
OVER — MAYBE ?

MUM BEING ILL

illness

crying

Being sad

dreams

being afraid

feelings inside
me

things I can't
talk about

sad things

things I
might do

other things

HOW I FEEL OR
THINK

Pleased

happy

Nice

Ace

silly

naughty

stupid

angry

sad

Lonely

worried

Jealous

hate it

sliders

Child may wish
to add words

More feelings
the longer the
card

Sliders. These may be used to
facilitate talk, and to direct talk.

anxiety. She did settle the slider window over that item on several occasions. When using the feelings-slider we were usually discussing some event, and then I would ask the child to show how this made her feel.

This child had certain attachment problems and also ambivalent feelings concerning her mother as well as very negative feelings towards her sister. The possibility of separating from her mother either because of the mother being ill or the child herself becoming ill took up a lot of her mental energy. It was helpful to zone in on the deeper feeling-slider material by first using the subject-slider dealing with 'Favourite things'.

As I explained in Chapter One when talking about direct work with Wendy, some children find it easier to write something down and pass it to the worker, just a single sentence which opens up an area for talk and investigation. I have therefore made use of what we call the mail-box or post-box (Figure 19). This sort of thing is quite easy to make out of a small cardboard box. The box may be covered with colourful wrapping paper. It needs to have a lid so that it resembles a cube. Then a slit for 'posting' notes is cut in the top and a little door is cut in one of the sides. The box is left with the child who is told that she may write a little note to the adult if she wishes, and just say who or what she would like to talk about next time they meet. With some children this has been very helpful and I have found short but pertinent little notes such as "I want to talk about my Mum again", or simply "about our Joe".

Another barrier breaking device is the *Talk-About-Card* (Figure 20). This looks a bit like the sociogram method. However, its use is quite different, and its main purpose is to get the ball rolling when children have perhaps only just come into care, or they are starting on some new phase because of some disruption and the whole of their life must feel in a terrible mess to them. As well as helping discussion it also helps the child to feel that the adult is not going to leave him in isolation. Again, I introduced this game in Chapter One when discussing work with Wendy. I say to the child "There must be lots of people you would like me to go and see, or you'd like to talk about, or maybe you'd like me to help you to write a letter to, so we'd better put their names on one of these coloured papers and stick them on this board. But first we must put a colour for you on the board. Which colour shall we choose for you?" The child then sticks his chosen colour in the middle of the board. We are using symbolism again of course. Instead of coloured paper for the child we could use a photograph of him or her.

Then he may want to feel that I will go and see Nana and Grandad and tell them how he is and post a letter or take one to them. As I am promising to keep child and grandparents informed of each other's progress they must have a colour chosen for them. A coloured joining up line or path is then made from the child's coloured square (circle or star, etc.) to the grandparents. Sometimes the children add various little decorative additions to these pathways. Children have asked me to stick on labels for previous

FIG. 19

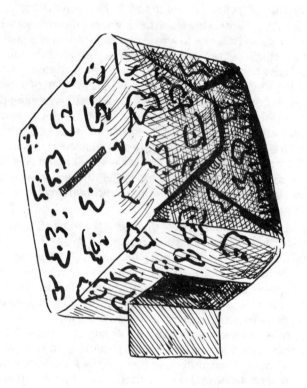

POST or MAIL BOX. This can be easily made from a cardboard box covered in gift wrapping paper

FIG. 20

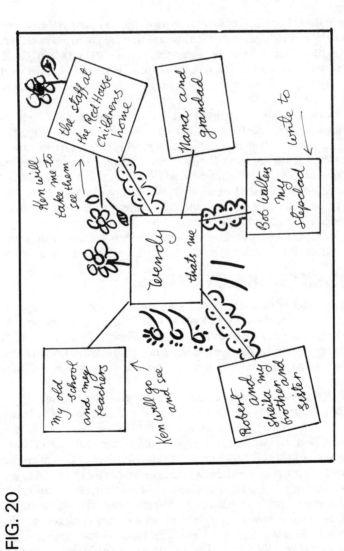

The 'TALK ABOUT' Card. We drew the straight lines connecting Wendy to the people she was concerned about. She decorated it herself. Note that at this stage she could not talk about her mother, it was too painful.

Children's Homes they've been in, for schools they've attended, and school teachers they've known.

It doesn't always follow that the desire expressed by the child when working on the Talk-About-Card is going to be met. In Wendy's case, for example, she wanted to re-establish contact with her step-father and half-siblings. As I have explained, the step-father's new wife would not permit this and so she had to settle for something less. Nevertheless, setting it out in this way helped her and me to identify and *deal with* a problem area in her relationships.

Sometimes the child will not put in a label for the very person the worker knows he or she is grieving about. For instance, the child who has been hurt by being separated from a parent may refuse to put the label on for the parents. It may be too painful at that point in time. There may be some mental blocking going on there which presently will have to be released by other opportunities to talk.

My final example of a barrier breaking device for young children is the ordinary glove puppet. This happy little idea has been used very effectively. Young children will often more easily and readily talk with the puppet than the adult on some subjects. When I use one I don't just put on a puppet show. No, the child *and* the puppet and I are doing something together such as sticking objects into the Life Story Book or painting pictures. The glove puppet is known by his name, and (s)he chips in on the conversation and has ideas (some of them silly) about how the painting or whatever should be done, and before we know where we are (s)he is definitely part of the scene, a real live partner to be answered when (s)he asks a question.

DISCUSSION-DIRECTING:

I have already touched on the idea of guiding the 'talk' along certain paths. Before closing this chapter I will look at two examples of *Discussion-Directing* devices. Since I have already described one of these devices, the Subjects-Slider, under the barrier breaking heading I shall start with that method, but now I shall be looking at it with a view to directing the conversation.

Obviously it is possible to have sliders already made with a list of subjects which might be discussed with anyone. The slider then might include subjects common to the life experience of all children such as school, games, dreams, Mum, Dad, and so on. In my experience, however, it is usually better to make a separate list for each child, otherwise, for direction purposes, the list is too broad and general. I always leave spaces for the child to add subjects to the slider. The adult should more often than not have certain aims in mind when working with a child. For this reason it is important to be able to put subjects down which would not appear in any general list, subjects such as 'Auntie Mabel and Uncle Jim' (short-term foster parents) or 'running away' or 'William and Steve' (the child's siblings). These of course go in amongst subjects of a more general nature.

The child is invited to run the slide window up or down to choose any subject to talk about (or to draw pictures about, etc). But it is usually a good idea to agree to 'turns' so that the worker and the child clearly have turns of choosing the subject. In this way we are able to pick the direction up in what feels like a rather democratic arrangement. Of course children may still block, but then our learning about their blocking is very important. Do not force the pace if the child blocks. You may have touched on something sensitive, if not painful — leave it for now.

I have also mentioned our second method of discussion-directing. This was when we were looking at barrier-breaking. I mentioned the use of discussion cards. We could call them 'talk cards'. Discussion cards are very useful, particularly for older children who are able to read them or put something down on the blank ones provided. However, for children who cannot read, picture cards can be made. People don't have to be expert artists to do this. In fact the child herself can be brought into this part of the work. A young child may be asked to draw a picture of Nana's house on a (largish) card, and even if it looks like an igloo it will forever more be 'Nana's house'. The worker can say "I'll draw you when you were a baby" and that will often be accepted as such. Those cards may then be used in a pack so that when the worker wants the talk to be round the early months of the child's life he picks out the baby picture. On the following pages I show a set of cards which was used first with a nine-year-old child and, with modifications, has been used for other children. There were four sets, each set of cards trimmed with a different colour. The sets were 'Family' (i.e. the child's natural family), 'School', 'Children's Home', and 'Behaviour'. These were all subject areas which contained problems or unresolved confusion in the child's mind. So I could either mingle the cards, select a few from each and let the child select, or use them at different times to talk round the particular subject of the set:

CHILDRENS HOME	CHILDRENS HOME	CHILDRENS HOME
Other children in 'Tall Trees'	Punishments	Staff and me
CHILDRENS HOME	CHILDRENS HOME	CHILDRENS HOME
sad thoughts I have	Visitors	Social worker and me
CHILDRENS HOME	CHILDRENS HOME	CHILDRENS HOME
Things that upset me	Things I like	

FAMILY	FAMILY	FAMILY
Visits and holidays	Nanna and Grandad	My Mum

FAMILY	FAMILY	FAMILY
things I think about	my brother and sister	why am I not at home?

FAMILY	FAMILY	FAMILY
would it work if I went home?		

JUST ME!	JUST ME!	JUST ME!
"No I won't"	Fab tales	Come here! Go there! do that! do this!

JUST ME!	JUST ME!	JUST ME!
"You can go first"	tall stories	"they always blame me"

JUST ME!	JUST ME!	JUST ME!
"take that"! and that"!	"I love ...."	"I hate ...."

SCHOOL	SCHOOL	SCHOOL
What other children say	TEACHERS: What they say to me	School meals? or packed lunches?

SCHOOL	SCHOOL	SCHOOL
School work	TEACHERS and ME	Favourite things

SCHOOL	SCHOOL	SCHOOL
School friends		

Looking at the 'Just Me' or 'Behaviour' set of cards it is easy to see that this child was experienced by many people as *bossy,* so we get the 'come here, go there, do that, do this' card. She was also being *aggressive,* so we find the 'take that and that' card. Like many of our children she was also prone to boast and fantasise, which annoyed many children and adults she met with, so we find the 'Fab tales' and the 'tall stories?' cards. The reader will also notice cards which had 'acceptable' behaviour patterns on them or 'praiseworthy behaviour'. The worker might use them to highlight such a piece of behaviour by the child. The cards must not be used to intimidate or to eliminate individual thrust but to open up 'talk' so as to help the child to think about her behaviour in relation to other people, and to obtain her view of her behaviour and the behaviour of others. Bear in mind that there may well be a stage with some disturbed and resentful children when I would, for the time being, avoid a role in which I dealt with 'right' or 'wrong' behaviour.

At the beginning of this chapter I said that the 'interview' situation should be avoided as much as possible during direct work. I gave an outline of the main aims. I named nine aims (a) to (i) involved in the process called direct work, and I said that in order to facilitate communication intended to meet these aims various 'games', devices or instruments may be used. So far I have enlarged on four of these aims and associated third objects and methods. These are, *Starters, Focussing on Life Trail, Barrier-Breaking* and *Discussion-Directing.* In the following chapters I shall discuss the remaining five aims and the techniques for meeting them whilst also considering attachment and bonding, social perception and planning as these relate to the task of direct work with children.

CHAPTER THREE

Communicating with Children — Some more ideas

In this chapter I shall introduce ideas and games I have found helpful when working with children who needed to explore and clarify certain social and relationship contexts of their lives. These explorations will include relatively pragmatic questions such as "What will the difference be if I am adopted rather than fostered?" But they will also include the complex psychology of relationships, "I don't know why I hate my dad but I do hate him".

I shall also talk about ways of helping child and worker to focus on the child's feelings or feeling states such as anxiety, anger, likes and dislikes.

Finally, we shall take a look at some of the devices I have found helpful when it was felt that the child needed to learn to change his patterns of behaving. This will include examples of children who were required to learn to relate in a different way to other people.

CLARIFYING SOCIAL AND PSYCHO-SOCIAL ASPECTS

You remember Peter, the child I spoke about in Chapter Two where neither foster parents nor child felt able to discuss certain basic feelings concerning their relationships. I'll take his situation again as I feel there were some rather clear examples where *third objects* were used in order to help him (and me) to clarify ideas and to reach decisions as a result. This was the case where the child's own social worker also found it difficult to get Peter to communicate, and where I used the dice football game as an 'ice-breaker'.

Although the methods I used concerning this child seem simple and clear, the case itself involved very complex and stressful relationships and an intolerable situation for Peter. This is not the place to discuss the full history of his stay in the foster home, nor the merits of the decision-making involved. The situation presented to me, however, was briefly this:

Peter had been in the foster home from about the age of two years. A younger brother had joined him about a year after his own placement. These two children had been brought up *mainly* in this foster family along with the four children of the foster parents (who also cared for 'short-stay' cases). In my judgement these particular foster parents were not suited to give Peter long-term care, and mixing long and short-term only made matters worse. However, there was a further complication in that Peter had not only remained in touch with his natural mother but went to stay with her and his step-father every other weekend, and for longer periods during holidays. Although there are strong arguments for keeping children in touch with their kith and kin such arrangements have to be worked out properly and the foster parents have to be able to relate satisfactorily to the child's parents and vice versa.

In Peter's case the situation had gone all wrong and he had become something of a pawn in a game played by the two opposing sets of caregivers, neither of which could be said to approach the epithet 'good enough' parents. The brutal facts of the situation included a demand by the foster parents for the child to 'decide' to give up them or his mother and step-father. The situation between the adults could not be mended and the longer this damaging psycho-social situation lasted the more harm would be done to the child. Fortunately I was able to establish a good working relationship with both sets of caregivers. Finally I employed two devices to help Peter and me in decision-making. These of course came at the end of other work not discussed here.

First, a simple 'double list' was worked out with Peter (Figure 21) which gave the foster parents' name at the head of one set of pros and cons ("better"/"worse") and his mother-stepfather surname at the head of the other set. This sort of list-making was possible with this particular child who could write and read well and was of normal intelligence. He had previously been too screwed up to talk, and also he'd been unable to say what he felt because of his loyalties to *both* sets of caregivers. It will be noted from Figure 21 that although material standards were poor in the home of his mother and stepfather, his psycho-social life was not so stressful.

The other device used was designed especially to help Peter obtain a clearer mental picture as a result of a set of diagrams. These diagrams are shown in Figures 22a to 24b and reveal the possible arrangements open to Peter. He could stay where he was (Figure 22a) which would mean virtually losing contact with his natural mother, or (Figure 22b) go and live with his natural mother and step-father. In this case he would be allowed to visit the foster parents frequently (both sets of caregivers accepted this). He could be found a new foster family and then (Figure 23) keep in touch with both previous sets of caregivers, or he could decide to make his home exclusively with one or other of the present caregivers (Figures 24a and b) losing touch with the other set.

Of course no child should be put into such a situation, but the facts were that Peter was in that situation and needed help in resolving it. In work-

FIG. 21

My foster family		My first family	
+ Better	– Worse	+ Better	– Worse
Moore comfort	Feel frightened	I like my step-dad here a lot.	Not so many comforts. Sometimes I'm not sure of the right things to do.
Nice holidays	Not sure what is the right thing to do so I get into trouble	Like going on the ice-cream round with him.	
Other children to play with	Could not be able to see my first Mum and stepdad if I stayed here.	I laugh much more.	
I like my grandad in this family		I feel nobody is watching me all the time.	
		I like my name. He was a cheat and plays with me. Nice holidays. Friends to play with.	

Peter's "double list"

FIG. 22**a**

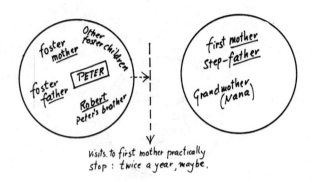

Visits. to first mother practically
stop : twice a year, maybe.

FIG. 22**b**

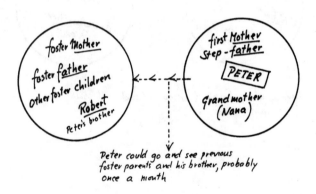

Peter could go and see previous
foster parents and his brother, probably
once a month

FIG. 23

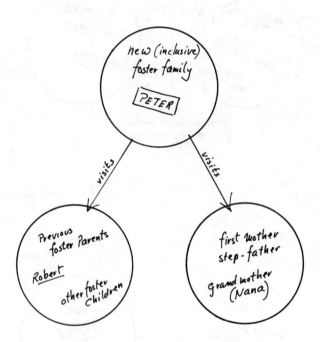

Peter would be able to keep in touch with both sets
of previous caregivers

FIG. 24a

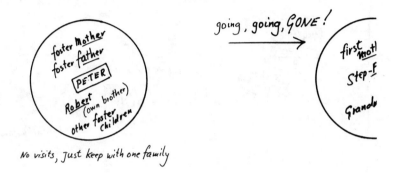

foster Mother
foster father
PETER
Robert (own brother)
other foster children

going, going, GONE!

first mot
step-F
Grand

No visits, just keep with one family

FIG. 24b

FIG. 24b

1other
er father
ert
wn brother)
er children

going, going, GONE!

first Mother
step-father
PETER
grandmother (Nana)

no visits, just keep with one family

FIG. 25

First stage: putting names of family members on a large sheet of paper

FIG. 26

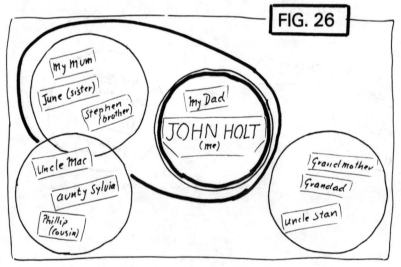

Second stage: drawing lines round the family groups

ing with children we have to take into account the actual *possible* arrangements. It may well have been that the Local Authority having the care of the child (on a Court Order) would not have agreed to Peter's going back to the care of his natural mother, and so the *possible* arrangements had to be established first.

Before reaching the stage discussed above, a similar device had been used to help Peter think and talk about where he wanted to live, or where he felt he 'belonged' as between the two sets of caregivers. First, I showed him some work done by an imaginary child, John. This child started the exercise by simply writing his own name more or less in the middle of the page. Or perhaps he'd stuck his name in, using a small self-adhesive label with his name written on it. Then he'd taken other labels with other 'names' on them, the names 'My Mum' and 'My Dad', 'Stephen' and 'June', his siblings, and so on (Figure 25). These he'd stuck in family groups. He drew a circle round each family. Then he and the worker talked about "Which family do you feel you want to live in and grow up in?" and he had put a special thick line made with a thick coloured felt pen round himself and his father and step-mother (Figure 26). But later in their discussions he'd added a line which went right round *two* families, his own with his dad and step-mother, and the family comprising his first mother and his siblings because he felt that in a way 'we all belong together'.

When Peter was invited to do this he found it easy to put in the groups of names. I suggested that he should put his own name in the middle of the page and the two family groups (foster family and first mum and step-father family) on each side of him. But the next part of the exercise stumped him I wanted to help Peter to express his wish by drawing a line round a group which would include one of the family groups and himself, and in this way express his idea about the family he 'belonged' to. But Peter was unable at that stage to do this. In the end I suggested the arrangement shown in Figure 27 where this unfortunate child hung on to both families! Peter was eventually able to select the arrangement shown in Figure 22b and to return to the care of his natural mother.

It would, of course, have been possible for me and the care agency to determine that the foster family was unsuitable and that there was little or no true attachment or bonding by child or foster parents and therefore to have arranged to move him, even to return him to the care of his natural mother without any in-depth discussion with the child. To take it right out of his hands, and to decide for him. This might have worked, but I feel that Peter did far better as a result of being involved, at twelve years of age, in the decision-making as regards his future care.

Doll's House Play:

Since this book is mainly concerned with the preparation of children for long-term placement in families (including the natural family), we have

FIG. 27

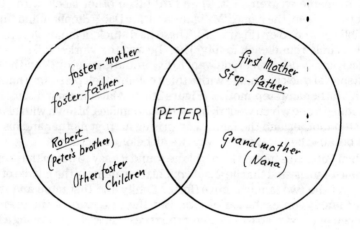

foster-mother
foster-father

Robert
(Peter's brother)

Other foster
Children

PETER

first Mother
step-father

Grandmother
(Nana)

not included chapters on psychotherapeutic work as such. However, apart from the fact that the direct work experience is in itself often very therapeutic, it should be appreciated that the techniques and devices used in the sort of direct work we are discussing lend themselves to therapy work. In Chapter Four we shall consider the use of direct work techniques when the objective is to provide the child with an enriched nurturing experience, enabling him to overcome sensory and emotional disadvantages. Several of the examples I give below, in which the immediate objective was to clarify some social or psychosocial aspect, have been drawn from cases which were referred primarily for therapy or where it was found that preparation had to include a specific therapeutic element.

As well as wonder and inquisitiveness, children have a marvellous potential for imagination. Yet this often remains undeveloped. I like to make use of devices which call upon the imagination of the child for much of their usefulness. As well as serving my direct purpose these imagination experiences can be exhilarating for children. Obviously, the application of any of these devices needs to be matched to the child and her ability or willingness to make use of it. For example, I make frequent use of dolls' houses and people (dolls or cut-out people) to go along with them. Sometimes I use only part of a doll's house because these dolls' houses can, in many cases, be taken to pieces since they are often made out of cardboard boxes — two at the bottom for the ground floor and two or more above for the upstairs rooms. The children often enjoy making these houses. We don't need to have sophisticated wooden or plastic commercially made things. They can take all the fun out of life.

Carl was another child who had to move from a foster home and who was helped with doll's house play. It is a great pity that so many of the children I am describing had foster family breakdowns (*disruptions*, to use our current terminology), but the fact that I am having to write about such children should help to underscore the need for preventive social work (keeping children in their own families) followed, if that is not feasible, by expert selection and preparation of alternative families and good preparation of the child. Another danger these days lies in the use of 'short-term' foster homes for long-term children. All sorts of problems arise from this usage. Carl's situation was partly caused by such a short-term placement.

Carl's older sister and younger brother attached themselves to the foster parents. After nearly a year the agency was still intimating that the children would be moving to their 'long-term' placement, when a suitable family was found. However, because of the bonding of the family with Carl's siblings, the agency rightly decided not to move them again. But the foster parents (not selected in the first place for a highly disturbed child like Carl) felt unable to go on caring for him. In fact it would have done harm to Carl and his siblings if any further efforts to 'bolster things up' had been made. So the difficult decision was made to move one child of a sibling

FIG. 28

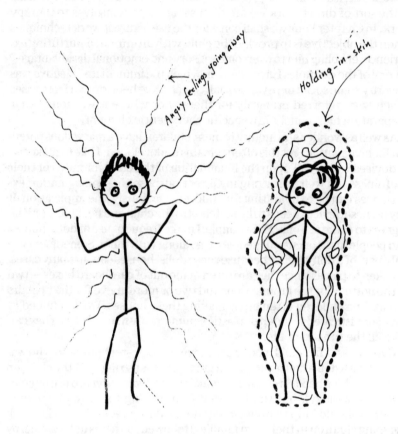

Angry feelings going away

Holding-in-skin

group of three — not a decision to be taken lightly.

Before using the doll's house with Carl on his own, I read to him the cartoon story of Mint, the kitten, published in John Fitzgerald's book (1983). This is about a kitten who, like most kittens, has to leave his first mum and then goes to live with a very nice lady, but has to move *again*. The reason for this second move (disruption!) is that the nice lady can't stop sneezing and of course it turns out that this is because of her being allergic (it's explained in simple language). So it's not *her* fault and it's not *Mint's* fault, it just didn't work out. This story produced a bit of discussion about *children* moving to new families.

After that I used two of the cardboard box rooms to represent two houses. With the cardboard cut-out figures I acted two or three small scenes, one of them taking place in the house that had no children and where the married couple were saying how much they wished they had a little boy. Eventually, the cut-out child named Carl (all the others were given names different to the real family) went to live with the childless couple. Then the cut-out children made visits to each other's houses. By the time the end of the 'play' was reached the real Carl was talking quite easily about a real move. Remember, he was already unsettled in the family.

Later his siblings joined us and we told them that Carl would eventually be going to a new family, and would they please watch while the play was acted again. This time all three children joined in and got quite carried away. They made bits of 'sadness' come in as well as 'happy things'. Of course that was not the end of the preparation. A lot of work had to follow. However, from then onwards it was open talk about the new family being found for Carl. In the weeks that followed he drew pictures *about* his new mum and dad and did other things, all aimed at helping him and his siblings to prepare for his move.

So here I was using a third object at a very difficult point in the child's life. Its use not only helped Carl but also helped me to observe the reactions of his siblings to the proposed move, and it helped them as well. The third object was a rather tatty collection of cardboard box doll's house rooms and some cardboard cut-out figures, some of them cut from magazines and pasted on to cardboard.

Anger Work.

All sorts of materials, play materials, come in as third objects which might be used as media for dealing with social and psychosocial aspects of the child's life. I have already explained how Daniel, in Chapter One, made a 'play-doh' face of his mother and then attacked it.

When working with children who have bottled-up anger I sometimes need to help them see that it is alright to express their anger, and that there are helpful and unhelpful ways of expressing anger. In fact I find that some children need a two-pronged form of treatment. As part of preparation they need to be able to talk about their anger being bottled up, but they nearly always require an active therapeutic outlet as well. So in addition to the symbolism of the games used in my direct work, I have usually involved children in climbing hills, digging holes, punching punch-balls and even in specially designed indoor games such as bombarding each other (sometimes bombarding me) with table tennis balls. Some children need to learn that it is safe to express their anger. They have learnt that to express anger is to invite rejection, so they may present themselves as too good to be true. They are over-controlling themselves in some ways.

Figure 28 shows a picture I have sometimes drawn in order to help a child understand about 'bottling feelings up'. These might be angry feelings but I could just as easily depict 'frightened' or 'scary' feelings or bereavement feelings, or any other feelings which the child may hold back rather than talk about or express in some other way.

The picture, drawn in very simple lines, shows two people. One of them has 'angry talk' coming out of him, shown by red wavy lines. These waves go out and are dissipated. The other person (the child in question maybe) has a thick green line encapsulating him. All his angry feelings are swilling about inside this capsule. The capsule is made by the person's 'holding-in-skin'.

I sometimes ask if the child is wearing his holding-in-skin, and we talk about how much better he might feel if he 'let out' some of his scary feelings by drawing a picture or talking about the scary things, or even by showing some anger. Then, if the child gets to being able to be angry and show it, we can move on to talk about how not to express anger and how to express anger.

You have to use your imagination so as to strike the right note of interest. Once, with a twelve year old boy who bottled up his anger and was very full of unexpressed hate, I was able to use a steam-driven model steam-roller to illustrate the point. On the boiler was a steam safety valve so that when the pressure rose beyond a certain point this steam-roller 'let out a bit of anger'. And of course, we could ask 'what would happen if it did not let off little bits of controlled steam?' The answer was that it might very well explode!

Owen and Curtis (1983) describe several techniques which might be employed in 'Anger Work'. All of them employ very simple equipment. But I would again emphasise the need to know how to cope with and help the caregivers to cope with, the child's anger once he or she feels free to express it. This is why the inexperienced worker must have supervision or consultation.

Dreams.

Don't forget the importance of dreams in this work. Dreams will usually be reported as being 'funny' or 'frightening'. Sometimes they are described as 'nightmares'. However, dreams often reveal a symbolism and are symbolic of some real anxiety or fear or apprehension or worrying memory. A careful study of a child's dreams can help the worker to lead the talk round to what seems a worry area. Children will sometimes respond readily to an invitation to draw or paint a picture of their dream. It is important to understand the symbolism of dreams. Often a child will report a 'nasty' dream in which he or she is attacked by a person or people. But the real anxiety may be about some non-physical or non-person factor. It may be an underlying anxiety that some *event* (e.g. illness of single parent) will 'attack' the family. At other times the symbolism is more direct and obvious such as the ten year old who dreamt of his mother turning into a witch. In reality there was a mixture of care and rejection on the part of the mother toward this child.

How Things Are.

When using direct work in connection with the social or psychosocial situations involving the child we are more often than not exploring or trying to explain how things are. In this work it is helpful if the worker can invent and even extemporise in a situation where she needs to come up with something very quickly. On one occasion I had understood that an eight year old girl would be attending a case conference about herself, and she had also understood this, but because of some misunderstanding she had not been brought from the Children's Home. I knew that the child was desperate to know not only what important decision had been made about her future, but how the decision was arrived at and how reasonable or otherwise it was. But she'd missed the case conference which she had been told she would be able to attend and to 'have a say'. The next best thing, better than merely reporting to her what had happened, was to act the case conference. I quickly collected an assortment of small articles such as an empty medicine bottle, a cardboard sweet carton and similar miscellany, labelled them with the names of the people who attended the conference, and then went off to see the child and to '*act*' (using my bottles, etc.) a play of the conference. Although at times she did get terribly agitated through frustration, she did in a way join in and argue certain points.

Many of the devices mentioned in Chapter Two may be used for the purpose of helping the child to deal with social and psychosocial aspects of his life and present situation. The eco-map or sociogram is an obvious example. Sliders may also be used for this purpose.

It is quite easy to design 'special' devices or games for a particular child and then to find that these have a general use since many other children can be helped with the same device.

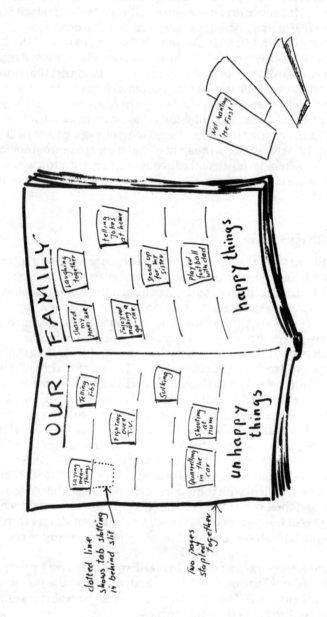

FIG. 29

The following five examples, all referred to very briefly, were originally used during some therapy work with a child, Alexander, who had very specific problems. The ideas have been found useful in working with other children.

First, here is a way of helping children to show the worker, and themselves, something about the balance of 'Happy things' and 'Unhappy things'. I opened a scrap-book at the two middle pages and wrote right across the top of the two pages 'Our Family'. Then on the left hand page I had the heading 'Happy Things' and on the right hand page the heading 'Unhappy Things'. On each page I made slits, twelve on each. A number of discs or tabs were then made, and on these were written a number of 'Happy Things' and a number of 'Unhappy Things' which were already known to me but which fluctuated. I was aiming of course to reduce the 'Unhappy Things'. Figure 29 shows this method. As usual, some tabs were left blank for things to be added. Alexander would choose appropriate tabs which he felt represented how things were at that time in his home life.

With the same child I was interested in helping him to develop a conscience about kind and unkind behaviour in himself. So I used the idea of a pair of old fashioned scales (Figure 30). Again I had a number of small cards, some with kind or helpful actions written on them, others with unhelpful or unkind actions, and some left blank. I knew a fair bit about the unhelpful and unkind things the child was doing, and of course the idea was not in any way to crush his spirit but to discuss round this behaviour and to help him express himself in a better way or to obviate the need for his hurtful actions, if necessary by getting some other member of the family to behave differently. But as well as inviting the child to carefully consider the list of negative actions we were careful to ask him also to see if any of the positive, helpful actions also belonged to him. I should say that there was absolutely no danger of my producing a priggish or conceited child. The other point to remember is that it did not matter if what I was getting back from the child was not always 'correct' in terms of the true situation. It served to stimulate 'talk' on these matters. Also Alexander recognised an ongoing aim to bring the scales down on the righthand, 'positive', side over the weeks of using the scales. We had a score scale on this side but not on the negative side.

The third game used in helping this child explain the situation to me was a series of little cut-out cardboard rings of various sizes from about six to twenty centimeters in diameter. Alexander had developed a genuine phobia concerning his younger half-brother, Billy. He could not tolerate this child anywhere near him. This was not just dislike, it was a true phobia so that if the younger child unthinkingly leaned across to borrow the scissors and suddenly came within touching distance of his brother, the older boy, Alexander, might react in the way most people would if a poisonous snake were suddenly placed on them. I wanted to discuss this

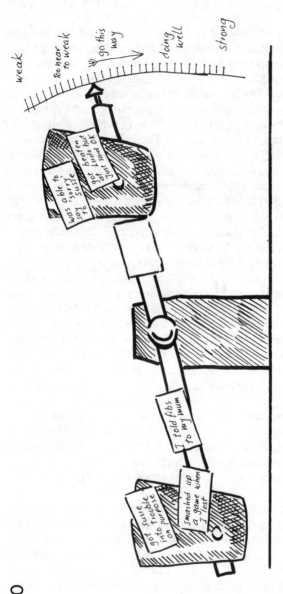

FIG. 30

FIG. 31

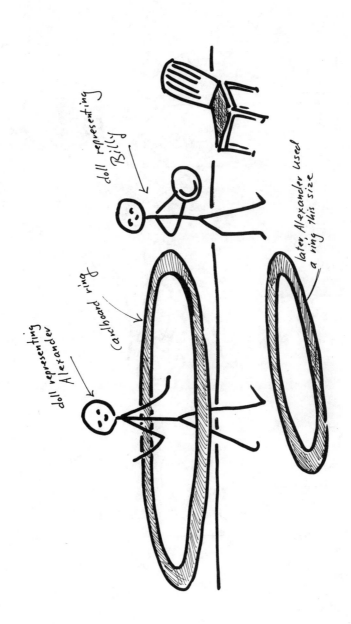

doll representing Billy

doll representing Alexander

cardboard ring

later Alexander used a ring this size

FIG. 32

painful phenomena with Alexander and to find ways of reducing it. One way of helping him to explain it was by using the cardboard rings and little model children 'Alexander and Billy'. I also stood a few of our homemade doll's house chairs in the 'room' marked out on a flat board (Alexander wouldn't play with dolls' houses!). Alex, as he was known, was asked to choose the ring which was 'safe' and place it round the model representing himself (Figure 31). This gave me some idea of how far out from Billy this strange feeling was supposed to be effective. Over the months of working with Alex, and it took many months, the rings gradually became smaller.

The fourth and fifth examples of games used in helping Alex are in fact two samples of the same device which I call symbolic cartoon drawing. These cartoons can produce a lot of fun because you don't have to be an artist and you can sometimes invite the child to make a 'better' picture, or cartoon, than you have made, and when animals like ostriches or elephants are involved both adult and child can fall about with laughter. Alex had a feeling of stigma attaching to himself because he had a stepfather. If any other child in the neighbourhood referred to this, or if an adult strayed unwittingly during conversation into this area, Alex would either 'curl up' and withdraw or would lash out with his tongue, provided it was safe to do so. I needed to help Alex to adopt a different attitude. On the one hand he was not to go and 'trumpet' the fact every time anybody new to the family came along, but on the other he need not hide the fact as something disgraceful. He need not be like an ostrich and stick his head in the sand. In fact, he could take his place as an ordinary child along with others, and if he did not react in his withdrawing or vituperative manner no-one would really bother. So the cartoon (Figure 32) had three signs or symbolic representations; a trumpet with 'sound' coming forth, an ostrich with head in the sand — neither of these two patterns of behaviour was necessary, neither would work. The third sign was a row of little matchstick people all alike. If Alex could accept the status and relationship as being quite common and not something 'bad' he would become like one of the match-stick people in this respect, nobody would notice him as different.

Finally, as far as Alex and our work with him is concerned, Figure 33 shows the cartoon drawing of a completely dual-control automobile with two sets of pedals and even two steering wheels. Along with other games, I used this when helping Alex to look at what he and other members of his family were doing when they tried to control the family. Alex was able to laugh at the idea of the car being steered in two directions at once, but of course this is what was happening in the family.

All these games have been used to help children talk and think about how things are.

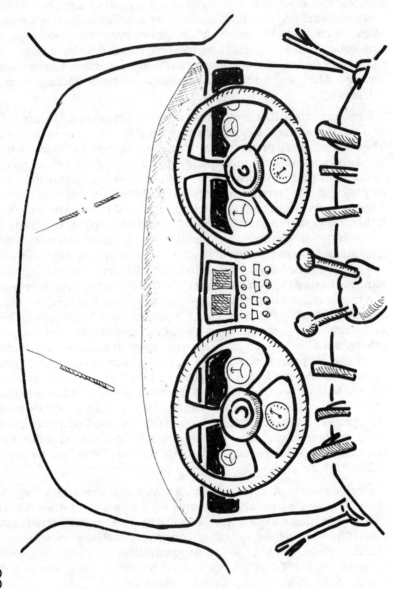

FIG. 33

Things that have changed but not changed.

Sometimes, dealing with a psychosocial situation means helping the child to come to terms with loss or with changes which have occurred in her life, but where the past is very much influencing the present. One of the most beautiful examples of the way in which ordinary things may help in this work is to be found in Owen and Curtis (1983). Here is a quotation from the booklet:

Loving and Caring Candles 1

OBJECTIVES: To enable the emotionally 'frozen' child to get in touch with the feelings of loss she experienced but avoided expressing when removed from the person(s) to whom she was attached and to provide the opportunity for the child to grieve for those lost people.

IMPLICATIONS: Will bring to the surface the grief surrounding the loss of the significant figures and the worker must allow these feelings full expression whilst supporting the child. The child may need physical comforting but some children are so damaged they cannot allow the worker too close and this physical contact may be limited to touching the hand, etc.

APPLICATION: Particularly useful in pre-placement work when the worker is enabling the child to come to terms with loss before moving on into a new family. Enables the child to 'Let go' of the past and move into the future, encouraging a readiness for attachment to a new family. This technique may be used following a visit by the child to a past home during which the worker became aware of unresolved feelings of loss which had previously gone unrecognised.

PREPARATION: A detailed knowledge of all the likely significant figures in the child's life.

EQUIPMENT: Two metal or tin-foil trays, candles (preferably coloured but not essential), material such as 'Plasticine' to hold the candles firmly upright on tray, matches, 'gentle' music on tape, tissues.

METHOD: 1. The worker explains that the candles represent the warm, loving and caring feelings we all have inside us for those to whom we have been close.
2. The worker lowers the lights and leads the child to talk about the person for whom it is felt the child needs to grieve.
3. The child is encouraged to choose a candle for that person, to stand it on one of the trays and to light it. In watching the candle glow and feeling the warmth of it, the child is encouraged to talk about her feelings for that person.
4. The child is asked to choose candles to represent the people with

FIG. 34

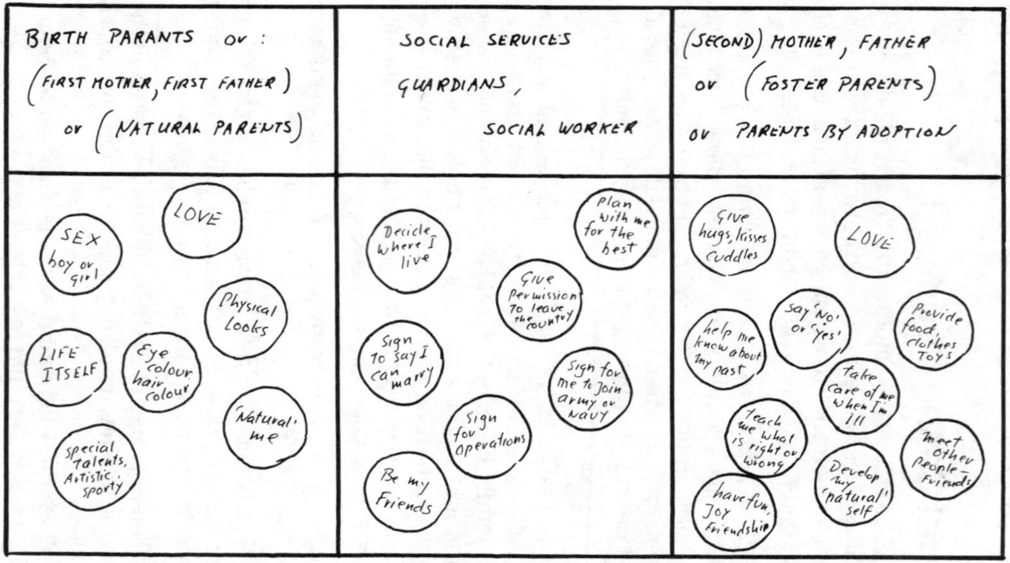

BIRTH PARENTS or: (FIRST MOTHER, FIRST FATHER) or (NATURAL PARENTS)	SOCIAL SERVICES, GUARDIANS, SOCIAL WORKER	(SECOND) MOTHER, FATHER or (FOSTER PARENTS) or PARENTS BY ADOPTION
LOVE; SEX boy or girl; Physical Looks; LIFE ITSELF; Eye colour, hair colour; Natural me; Special talents, Artistic, sporty	Plan with me for the best; Decide where I live; Give Permission to leave the country; Sign to say I can marry; Sign for me to join army or navy; Sign for operations; Be my Friends	LOVE; Give hugs, kisses, cuddles; Provide food, clothes, toys; Say 'no', or 'yes'; Take care of me when I'm ill; Help me know about my past; Meet other people, friends; Develop my (natural) self; Teach me what is right or wrong; Have fun, joy, friendship

In the case of an Adoption Order being made many of the discs could be moved from the middle column over to the third column.

whom she is now living and place them on the same try. She is encouraged to talk about whether or not she has lit candles for them. She may choose not to do so.

5. The worker explains that, as the child no longer lives with the first person, that candle should be moved to a different tray. The burning candle is moved to the second tray. This is placed at the other side of the darkened room, so symbolising the separation which occurred.

6. The child is encouraged to share her feelings about the separation and is held and comforted by the worker when appropriate.

7. The worker explains to the child that there are many people who pass through our lives for whom we will light loving and caring candles and that, if we are separated, these become memory candles which still burn bright, giving us a feeling of warmth and love even when we are no longer together. The worker helps the child to talk about this and see the value of having these good memories with us for always. At this time a cuddling session to soft music can be very pleasant and reinforce the session.

8. When the time is right, stage two can begin and the worker moves on to talk with the child about the future. She shows the child that it is not necessary to stop having loving and caring memories of one person before starting to love and care for another. The worker lights the candles representing the present caretakers and the child and the worker watch these and the original candles burning brightly at the same time but at opposite ends of the room.

9. The worker may wish to add a candle to each tray representing the feelings the adults have in their turn for the child.

10. The worker encourages the child to talk about the issues of having feelings for people and the consequences and possible risks for the child in doing so.

Sometimes there is a need to talk about very practical matters concerning, for example, the reasons for the child coming into care. These may seem like purely social or even administrative concerns, but nearly always there is a psychosocial element present. I borrowed an idea from Dr. Vera Fahlberg and constructed a board, divided into three sections and designed to help children talk about, and understand, the implications of being in care and of fostering or adoption, and to help them understand more about inherited characteristics, parental or caregiver responsibility, and agency responsibility.

The board (Figure 34) has three sections or columns which are headed in this way (alternative headings shown):

Birth parents	Social Services	Parents
First Mum	Guardians, Court	Second Mum and Dad
First Dad	Social Worker	Foster parents
Natural parents		Parents who adopted me

FIG. 35

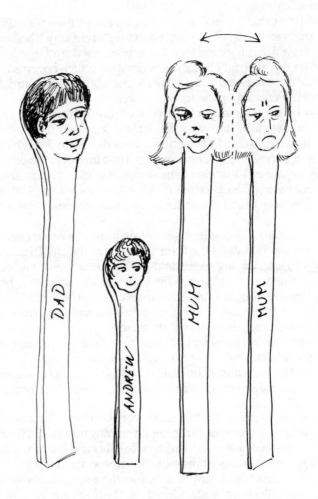

Simple cardboard spoon puppets with 'happy' and 'cross' faces.

A number of discs were made. On these I wrote characteristics and functions, roles and responsibilities, some of which relate only (and at all times) to the natural parents and the child, some to the caregivers and the child, and some which may reside with the social work agency whilst the child is in care but may later, if the child is adopted or returns to the care of a natural parent, reside with the adopted or natural parents. So, if we take certain things which were 'given' to the child by the first parents, we can have discs for 'eye colour, hair colour, tall, short, physical looks'. These can all go on one disc. Then I had a disc for 'Sex....boy or girl' and one for 'Life itself' and 'Special gifts or talents... artistic, musical'. These are characteristics (we say 'things' don't we) which have been given to the child by his or her parents. I do have more than one disc for 'Love' because I try to show, if I can, that the first parent gave the child love (or that some other caregivers gave love) and that the present caregivers are also giving this. Then I used discs which referred to things which may reside with the agency or in some cases with a court (as in wardship cases). These included: 'Consent for operations' and 'Decide where I live....agree to where I live' and 'Sign for my going in the army, navy or air-force'. The third set of discs have to do with the child in the family of the present caregivers. These include things like 'Give hugs, kisses, cuddles', 'Provide food, clothes, toys, etc.' 'Take care of me when I am sick', and of course 'Love'.

The worker may use the board in various ways. The discs of course may either be pinned onto the board or can be made to adhere by other means. The columns may be empty at the start of the session so that child and worker discuss the appropriate column before the disc goes in. On the other hand they could all be in place representing how things stand at that date and then, to show the child the difference (or some of the differences) between fostering and adoption, those responsibilities and roles which reside temporarily with the agency would be transferred to the 'Parents who adopted me' column. The heading 'Foster Parents' in that column could then be blocked out with a piece of card of the right size. For example I use a disc which says 'Give permission for me to get married'. This would come out of the agency column and go into the adopter's column.

For younger children puppet games may be helpful when reviewing with the child the reasons for coming into care. This question of coming into care frequently looms very large in the child's list of things he feels indignant or frustrated about, so it is not something to be brushed over or treated lightly. Many children feel they've been cheated and that the powerful authority of the courts or the Social Services Department has been ill-used against them. Puppets may be simply made in the form of 'spoon puppets' (Figure 35) as recommended in the booklet 'Finding Out About Me' (Familymakers, 1983), or you may prefer to use the glove puppets which can be purchased. An alternative to puppets is the doll's house figure, either simple cardboard cut-outs or real doll-figures you can purchase these days from toy shops.

There are many ways of making them enact the story of the child coming into care. Sometimes I find it helpful to make the figures talk to each other, enacting it as from the case file. Depending on the child, I have found it helpful for him or her to take the parts of themselves and their siblings and parents, while I 'act' the agency worker's roles. Then you can switch round and say 'You make this doll talk now because I may not have done it right'. Then you may see how the child views the roles played by the various key people on the agency side. Some children have been quite keen to 'act' the whole play whilst I sat and watched. The object of this play is to correct 'wrong' ideas and to provide the opportunity for the child to give his version, but we must be careful to have obtained an accurate as possible account of what did happen, *and* be alert to possible errors in our own account.

FOCUSSING ON THE EMOTIONAL.

The term 'Affect' is a general term used by psychologists and psychiatrists to refer to the feelings and emotions. In this section I shall describe games which I have used to help the child and me to talk about feelings or emotions such as fear, apprehension, anger, joy, sadness, happy-feelings, liking, hating, and so forth.

Games already described.

Many of the devices or games already described in this and the preceding chapter will lend themselves to work intended to help the child and worker to discuss feelings, and to express feelings. In fact such is the way these life experiences intertwine that I more often than not find myself dealing with several aspects when making use of a single device.

This was seen clearly in the last section when I looked at the work with the candles. I was then focussing on the clarification aspect, helping the child to 'see' how things were, but at the same time the child was being helped both by re-experiencing certain emotional involvements and by resolving emotional conflicts.

So, in this connection, I shall describe the use of feelings-sliders, discussed and illustrated in Chapter Two, and drawing and painting. The drawings shown in the illustrations (Figures 15(a)(b)) demonstrate that this medium may be used to focus the discussion on the child's feelings. Drawing and painting can of course be therapeutic in their own right. Some children and young people like to express feelings in the form of poetry. The worker is then able to admire the actual poetic efforts, so strengthening the child's confidence, and to use the contact for discussion or 'talk' concerning the feelings expressed in the poetry.

I have already talked about the importance of dream material. Dreams, however, are usually attached to some affective aspect of life and so become another source for focussing on the child's emotional or affective state.

In fact, this affective aspect of the child's life is so central to the damaged self-identity and the development of a healthier self-identity, that it is likely to emerge whenever direct work with children is undertaken. Feelings are likely to be involved when we are aiming primarily to focus, for example, on a plan for the child's future. Feelings are involved if we focus on the child's history and the reasons for his or her coming into care. This is why it is possible to use almost any of the devices discussed in this book when the principal objective might be to focus on feelings. But *much* of the discussion will be seen to centre round the child's and the adult's feelings towards each other. Again, when I discussed 'anger work' in a previous section the devices and techniques used in helping the child to express anger were also part of my stock of games and techniques used to help the child and me to focus on the emotional aspects. Dolls' houses, toy theatres, actual dressing-up and play-acting may all be used to help child and worker to focus on the affective.

It may be helpful to consider affective material as being handled by the worker and the child in two stages. Stage one is the *recognition* stage during which, while other objectives are being met in preparation and while use is being made of the various techniques for other reasons, such as clarification or life-trail, the child signals and the worker recognises the signals indicating that there is an emotional aspect involved. Stage two is where the worker, having recognised the possible emotional aspects, enables the child to express feelings about people, events, experiences and so forth, using techniques deliberately for this purpose. In practice these stages may often occur in immediate consecutive sequence because the experienced worker may feel able to deviate from the objective there and then in order to make use of the affective material emerging.

This happened during the session with the child who was making the sociogram or eco-map in Figure 16. Although the eight-year-old, as explained in Chapter Two, was building up a clear picture of his life history and the key figures involved in his life, the 'talk' suddenly became centred on his dreams. His feelings emerged. There was emotional or affective material surfacing so I allowed this to flow out and also got the child to stick the two flaps on the sociogram, one covering a list of 'Things I don't like' amd the other covering some brief statements about disturbing dreams he'd had.

Many children referred for preparation for long-term placement have intense behaviour-attached feelings which are complex and sometimes include attitudes or attitude clusters (i.e. inter-related attitudes) which might best be described as 'sense of' feelings. A child may come with a sense of rejection, or a sense of injustice, or a sense of guilt, or a sense of inferiority. But the behaviour patterns of the children will differ considerably, depending upon many variables. One child with a sense of rejection may be hostile, another may be withdrawn. These attitude clusters are very important. If we are helping a child to express anger it is just as important to know why he is angry. He may have developed a sense of injustice or inferiority as a result of the handling by previous caregivers, or ideas prevalent in the community. As well as being aware, therefore, of behaviour linked with the affective aspects of loss and deprivation generally, i.e. such feelings as anger, anxiety, fear, we must be alert to feelings of rejection, injustice, guilt and inferiority.

Often the child's behaviour will signal to the experienced worker that his emotional hurt is, so to speak, the opposite to his behaviour. The boasting, fantasising child may often have strong feelings of inferiority. He tends to over-compensate. Stigma is another reason for negative affective experience in a child. Stigma may be experienced as a result of feeling 'different' in some way. Ervine Goffman (1963) refers to stigma terms such as *cripple, bastard, moron.* But in our experience some children feel stigmatised if they are 'foster children' or even 'adopted'. Much will depend on the strength of the child's self-image. Kadushin (1970), however, points out that the coloured child placed with a white family needs a much stronger self-image, even in an accepting white family, because of stigma as society 'sees it'. Such a child may experience negative feelings associated with being *fostered* and *coloured,* a double stigma.

Behaviour-Change.

John Fitzgerald's book 'Building New Families' (1982) he outlines some cases, discussing the treatment and the progress made. Here are a few excerpts interspersed with my own comments. The excerpts taken together highlight changes in the child's behaviour from what would have been expected or forecast if treatment had not been available:

> 'As with Polly and Anthony, George's problems stemmed very obviously from the deprivations and traumas he had endured, and knowing a good deal about his past made it easier to plan a treatment programme for him. He was clearly defending himself against anxiety by being over-controlled, which meant that he could not let himself go to sleep and could neither accept help, nor confide in adults'.

Notice that Fitzgerald is talking here about *behaviour.* George was 'over-controlled' and could not 'let himself go to sleep', no could he accept help from or confide in adults. But of course Fitzgerald recognises underlying psychosocial causes and he states that George's problems (including the behaviour) stemmed from deprivations and traumas he had endured. Fitzgerald then goes on to outline the ways in which George was to be helped. Notice also that there is a definite plan which has an aim, in the same way

'The plan was to let George take his own time, to reach out to him in play and in neutral areas of daily life. To force the pace would be to strengthen his defences and make him feel even more vulnerable. We recognised that he might need to regress while he mourned the losses of his past....'

Now comes part of the 'plan' which involves the affective (emotional) as well as the behavioural and intellectual aspects of the child's personality:

'It was agreed that he should be gently encouraged to form an attachment to a housemother with whom he could let down his defences and begin to talk about his family and their treatment of him......We also recognised that George would probably have to reject his mother and stepfather before he would be able to take on a new family. On a practical level, he needed individual help with reading so as to ensure that his good potential was not overlooked.

Now we come to the first major change in his general behaviour:

'The first step forward was an improvement in his ability to trust adults'.

But besides *general* behaviour individuals exhibit detailed idiosyncratic behaviour in quite small things:

'At first when anyone indicated that they understood how he felt or tried to comfort him, he was very tense. His hand, when held, remained as unmoving as a block of wood and he was very sensitive to any type of correction, no matter how mild'.

The 'correction' he had been used to before going to St. Lukes, John Fitzgerald's place, had affected the way he related and *behaved*. This showed up clearly after an incident when George was mildly reprimanded:

He went out, but was found shortly afterwards standing in a corner looking very pale and frightened. The housemother suggested that if he wanted to cry it was all right to do so and she knelt down and held him in her arms. He burst into violent sobs and said: 'At the other house I was forbidden to cry'. After this it was easier for him to show his feelings.

Let me repeat, 'After this it was easier for him to show his feelings'.

That was a behaviour change, a change in his general pattern of behaving. It is difficult for us to remember that many of the children we set out to help have had to fathom out how to behave, how to interact with other folk when they have moved from placement to placement. George had 'learnt' not to cry. A little later we find still more behavioural change:

'The next improvement was his increasing ability to talk about his mother and stepfather'.

The story of George's improvement, his ability to cope with life and to develop acceptable patterns of behaviour continues so that we find Fitzgerald reporting:

'A gentle teasing relationship with one of the men on the staff helped him to release some aggression in an appropriate manner and to hold his own better in a group'.

Often, when children are being helped in this way, they need to regress in certain areas of their lives. We must understand this and be prepared for some forms of regressive behaviour. If these are handled wisely and without alarm, the child will grow out of such behaviour. So we find in George's case:

'As expected, George regressed in toilet training. He wet the bed for a while and had occasional accidents during the day!'

Gradually George is able to control his impulses and to change his interactive behaviour so that this in turn affects the way other people respond and behave towards him:

'Within a year he became much happier, relaxed and confident, and although he still had some difficulties with other children he was now accepted by them and able to play constructively. With adults he was discriminating, but had a warm relationship with several staff members.....'

George reached the stage in his preparation when he could be placed with a family. The final paragraph of Fitzgerald's account shows how George and children like him can overcome the trauma of earlier deprivation, and it also reminds us of the importance of preparation and support for the caregivers

'His placement went smoothly, but then he had a wild period of regression, during which the new family needed to draw on our experience of dealing with George in his early days at St. Lukes. After this he settled very well and his new parents found him a most lovable and rewarding youngster'.

Eventually, the child's behaviour will change as a result of the interaction between him, his new caregivers, and the other people coming into his life. But as we see from the experience with George, children can be prepared for placement in such a way that we get sufficient behaviour change to enable a placement to have a reasonable start. Transplanting is always a critical operation whether it be with plants, hearts or a whole child.

In Chapter One I spoke about a game I first played with Jamie, in fact I made the game up when I was working with him and discovered that I needed to discuss the *nature* of family-living with him. I called this *What is a Family*.

Figure 36 shows you the 'board' we played it on. In fact we had a large sheet of paper rather than a board. In the centre of the paper I left a space for the house since all families need a house to live in — this *becomes* their home. I could have drawn the house in already, or stuck it into position, but this would have defeated my objective. Remember that I usually make use of the *deflected discussion*, that is I chat with the child while he or she is engaged in some interesting but not too demanding task. So I wanted Jamie to be able to stick the house in and, if he wished, to crayon or paint it. He did this whilst we talked. Figure 37 gives you a close-up of the house. You see that it is drawn on a folded-over piece of paper so that the front of the house is on a flap which can be raised to reveal the interior, two rooms up, two down, hall and landing. I provided some little cut-out figures, Mum, Dad and two children and invited Jamie to stick these in, putting them into rooms of his choice.

One of the things I wanted to do was to enter into some kind of discourse with Jamie about the *value* of a good family life experience. Of course I could not use such an expression with him. I also wanted to talk about the way parents and children are expected to behave. Again, I couldn't use such language when discoursing with Jamie, but I wanted him to begin to see what a parent's role may be. So how could I do this?

You will see from Figure 36 that Jamie and I had to draw up several lists. The two most important were headed:

'How can families help children?' and
'How can children help families?'

Of course I knew that Jamie would start with practical helping tasks, things which he'd been told were things he should do. So I got statements such as:

'Children can help to do the shopping'

What I wanted to work round to, however, was something much deeper. Bit by bit, therefore, our 'talk' got round to other, deeper things so that after some time Jamie was able to say:

'Children can make families happy', and
'Children can give love'

Remember, this took weeks to get to. Jamie had *What is a Family* hanging up in his bedroom for weeks. Sometimes when I saw him we would spend ten to fifteen minutes with it, sometimes a bit longer.

The other important area for discussion was covered in the list headed:

FIG. 36

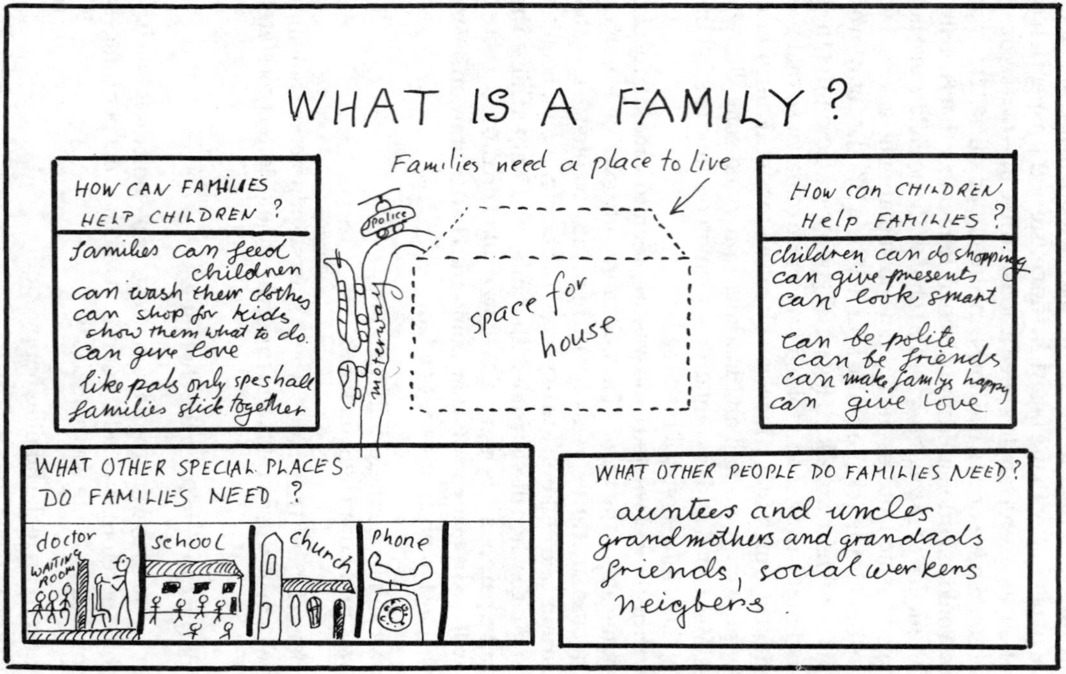
WHAT IS A FAMILY ?
HOW CAN FAMILIES HELP CHILDREN ?
families can feed children
can wash their clothes
can shop for kids
show them what to do.
can give love
like pals only speshall
families stick together
Families need a place to live
police
moterway
space for house
How can CHILDREN Help FAMILIES ?
children can do shopping
can give presents
can look smart
can be polite
can be friends
can make familys happy
can give love
WHAT OTHER SPECIAL PLACES DO FAMILIES NEED ?
doctor
WAITING ROOM
school
church
Phone
WHAT OTHER PEOPLE DO FAMILIES NEED ?
aunties and uncles
grandmothers and grandads
friends, social werkers
neigbers .

'How can Families Help Children?'

The answers given by Jamie started off again with obvious, practical tasks such as:

'Families can feed children'
'Wash their clothes'

All these came out whilst Jamie was crayoning or cutting out or involved in some other enjoyable past-time. I really felt we were getting somewhere when, towards the end of the preparation period, he was able to contribute:

'Families are like pals only special', and
'Families stick together'.

Of course, I've corrected the spelling where he actually wrote them in. Sometimes he got me to write down what he'd said.

Now have a look at the close-up of the family home in Figure 37. You will see that when Jamie stuck the cut-out of the little boy in, he put him halfway between the bed and the ceiling! The little boy was in fact using the bed as a trampoline for springing up and down. Here's how our conversation went over that point:

Me:	"Oh, I see, the little boy's having fun, is he?"
Jamie:	"Yes, he's bouncing about on the bed".
Me:	"I bet that's fun. How old is the little boy, would you say?"
Jamie:	"He's about six........"
Me:	"Six........poor old bed, it will get hurt".
Jamie:	"No, three, he's three........they've only got two bedrooms in this house....we had three".
Me:	"What if the little boy was about eight?" (Jamie's age).
Jamie:	"The bed would go bang, bump........where's the pen?"

Here Jamie took the pen and wrote in the room below, near the ceiling, 'bang' 'bump' as they do in the comics (see Figure 37).

Me:	"The boy's father is in that room downstairs, what's he going to say?"

Jamie sat back and looked at the scene for a while then said:

Jamie:	"He'd be mad......he'd get mad".
Me:	"Do you think he should get mad?"
Jamie:	"Yes, because the bed's getting bashed up".
Me:	"Would he be a good Dad if he didn't care and he just laughed?"
Jamie:	"No......it would be alright if it was a little boy......not a big boy".

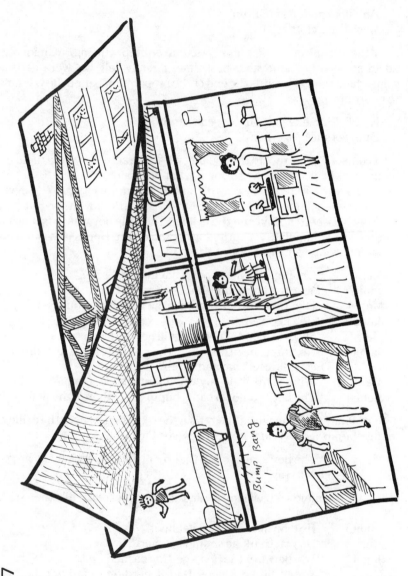

FIG. 37

So at this point Jamie and I were really talking about parental roles — maintaining order, training, looking after the home. Of course there were the roles of protection, supplying affection, helping children to become independent. Any of these could come out in discussion around some task or game, but at this point we were dealing with some very pragmatic roles and Jamie needed to sort these out in his mind since at that time he hardly accepted discipline or training from anyone.

The reader will observe (Figure 37) that Jamie pasted the mother next to the kitchen sink, a chauvinist touch perhaps! However, it led on to a chat about children having tasks to do and their attitudes about such tasks.

One of the lists shown on the *What is a Family* layout (Figure 36) had to be completed by drawing in pictures of 'Places' people and families need. In fact I suppose I was more interested in *services* such as schools, clinics, shops, etc., but as we've seen before, depending on the vocabulary and understanding of the child, one has to select basic or less-basic words.

In order to give Jamie the idea, I had already drawn in the shops and the doctor's surgery. After a bit of discussion during which I said 'Can you think of other places you will go to?' Jamie drew a school and a church. Then he put in a drawing of a telephone. He was obviously thinking of a service here. As a matter of fact he found it quite helpful to ring up different caregivers (Children's Homes' staff and foster parents) he'd been with previously.

It was Jamie's own idea to link these drawings up with the family home by drawing in a 'motorway' (Figure 36), complete with a police car.

I wanted to help Jamie to get the idea that when he went into a family, a nuclear family group, it would not be an isolated splinter group but would be linked into a network. In order to express this in the way a child could understand I wrote, for our fourth list:

'The Family is lonely if it is on its own — What Other People shall we give them?'

Jamie eventually came up with:

Aunties and Uncles.
Grandfathers and Grandmothers.
Friends.
Social Workers.
Neighbours.

Notice that Jamie saw nothing unusual in having 'Social Workers' included in the list.

'What is a Family' was made up for one child, an intelligent child who had certain needs, who had never remained long in any family except families which were dysfunctional. I have used the principle on several occasions since, but I have always tailored the game to the child I was work-

FIG. 38

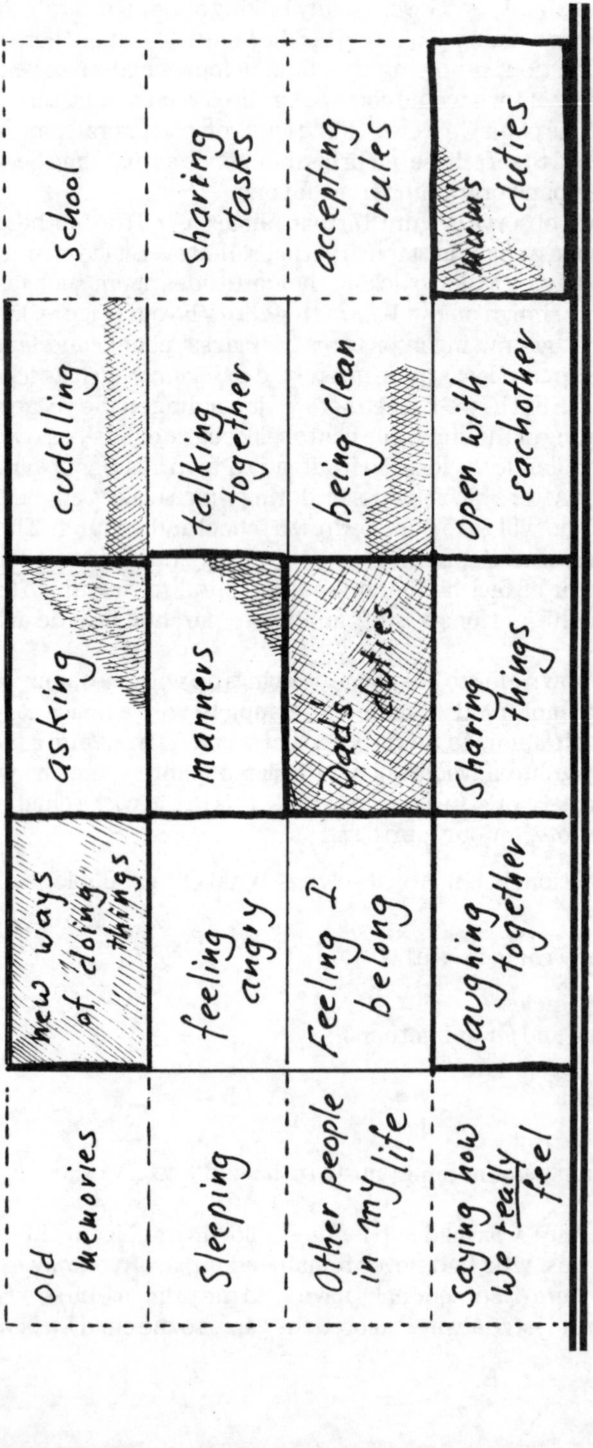

Old memories	new ways of "doing" things	asking	cuddling	School
Sleeping	feeling angry	manners	talking together	Sharing tasks
Other people in my life	Feeling I belong	Dads' duties	being clean	accepting rules
Saying how we really feel	laughing together	Sharing things	open with eachother	Mum's duties

The shaded portions show the bricks which have been worked on ing with. However, it is an example of a game or device used to help bring about changes in the behaviour, springing from the development of new ideas about roles and relationships, a very difficult area if we try relying on ordinary instruction.

One game I have found to be very helpful in attitude and behaviour change, especially during a period of introduction to a new family or during gradual rehabilitation to the child's natural family, is the game of *Building a Wall*.

The game has been described by Pat Curtis (1983) and lends itself to variations. Children who are moving into new families and have had unsatisfactory nurturing and training experiences need to *build* a relationship with their new caregivers. For that matter the caregivers also have the task of building a relationship.

This concept of building or adding-to is useful because the child does come to recognise that there is an effort, a task, and as we build up the bricks a feeling of achievement can result.

The bricks can represent relationship tasks such as 'sharing things' or 'saying how I really feel and saying it kindly'. They can represent attitudes which may need changing, such as 'accepting rules' or they may stand for the little behaviour particles such as 'laughing together' or 'cuddling'.

When a child is 'building a wall' with the worker, or with the foster parents or other caregiver, the usual method is to have a whole mixture of bricks. These bricks represent all these different tasks, functions and attitudes relating to family life which need to be discussed. Although the task or problem or whatever may be written-in, the actual brick is not in place until the adult feels that the subject has been dealt with sufficiently and where appropriate a positive change has occurred in the child's behaviour.

Figure 38 shows a wall being built. I used this with a child during the period of introductions. The actual 'things' to be talked about were decided by the child, the prospective foster parents and myself so that the child did not feel there was too much being imposed on him.

I have developed the idea of painting in half a brick where I felt there was progress but where we still needed to think further about that area of development. Another method was to get the child to stick in a full or half brick by using our coloured 'jollycraft' gummed squares.

You can try to put what you feel are the more important or basic topics at the ground level so as to get the feeling of building upwards, but this doesn't usually work out so I don't worry if the bricks take their place in mid-air!

This technique has been used with teenagers as well as younger children. It does help to have this sort of visual aid when working with children. Again, the wall becomes a monitoring device and helps the child to *see* or *feel* the progress, or otherwise, being made. I have spoken of 'building rela-

FIG. 39

The jigsaw pieces are labelled: Cuddles, Belonging, Dad's Responsibilities, saying how we feel, new ways of doing things, hobbies, School, sharing, talking, Mum's Responsibilities, accepting rules, open with eachother, laughing together, Remembering together, Tasks

Some parts of this re-usable jigsaw are left blank in case other subjects crop up tionships' but this technique of wall-building helps the child to make behavioural adjustments as a result of learning about acceptable standards and social customs or rules which he has missed-out on. Lots of the children I meet have simply *missed-out* on things. They may have missed-out on nursery rhymes when young, or on going shopping — 'ordinary things'. And of course they may be quite confused about parent or sibling roles.

So in my wall (Figure 38) you will see bricks labelled 'manners' and 'being clean' and 'Dad's duties'. But because I wanted to talk about 'being clean' it doesn't mean I wanted to produce a namby-pamby child. It was simply that having a bath was something unique and detestable to the particular child just going into a foster home. On the other hand, if he wasn't allowed to come in from a game of football with a liberal supply of mud the foster parents would need to change *their* ideas.

An alternative to the wall-building as a technique when helping children to make behavioural adjustments is the jigsaw puzzle (Figure 39). I have used jigsaws in a way similar to wall building but the advantage of the jigsaw, which should be made using fairly thick cardboard, is that the child and the worker can keep taking it to pieces and restructuring it.

Sometimes it is helpful to put the whole thing together, a simple form of amusement in itself, and then to extract the pieces you or the child or foster parent feel still need working on. This leaves you with a picture of how much progress has taken place since you last played the game. It becomes a monitoring device again. I have often divided a task between two pieces of the jigsaw as I felt it would give the child encouragement to have a part of the task shown as completed.

Personality Shields

Making shields can be entertaining, absorbing, and creative. They can also be used as third-objects for direct work with children. This game has been in use now for several years and seems mainly to have been adopted in order to help children look at, and maybe come to terms with, their own personality. To help them in establishing a self-identity.

Shields are fun because they are so adaptable. They can be nice and big. You can get the child to stick all sorts of materials and objects on them and he or she can really go to town with gaudy, flashy materials sewn, pasted or clipped on to the basic shield shape.

Most workers so far seem to have used shields mainly as a means of helping the child to project an image of his personality. So the shield may be quartered and then the quarters used for specific aspects of the child's personality. One quarter may show the child's age, physical characteristics and some other associated aspect. Another would display the child's 'favourite things' with maybe an example of favourite colour, or an actual pencil stuck on if 'drawing' is one of his favourite things, and so on with the other

FIG. 40

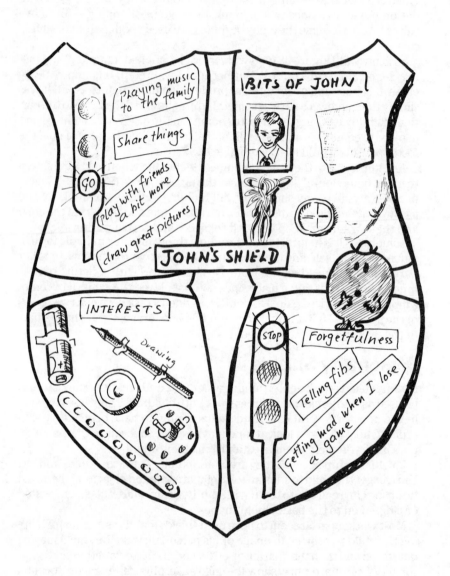

quarters.

I have made use of shields when helping to bring about a change in behaviour. In fact I used this idea with a whole family. This was a sort of family therapy game in which every member of the family made a shield, but all members of the family had ideas about what should go on other members' shields. Such a way of using the shield game does of course require someone well experienced in group work to act as therapist, or 'referee'.

Figure 40 shows one of the shields used in this way. It is quartered. The top right hand quarter has the words 'bits of John' written in above an odd collection of bits and pieces. These were just an assortment of things he liked or he'd had around for some time. They include a photograph of himself, a piece of cloth he liked because it had a 'nice smooth feel' about it, a key, and a clip of his hair.

The left-hand bottom quarter is headed 'interests' and has things which tell us about John's interests. He likes doing electrical things and wants to be an electrician so he has put a little battery on the shield. He likes doing mechanical things so he's fixed some pieces of mechanical model-making equipment on the shield. He also likes drawing and playing rather brainy games like draughts and chess so he's put a draughts piece on the shield.

But now we come to the special behaviour-change bits. The top left-hand quarter has some traffic lights with the green light for 'go' showing. In this quarter we put the kind of behaviour or activities which people found nice or helpful or positive about John. We want these to continue. It also has things we would like him to develop. So we find:

'Playing music to the family'
'Play with friends a bit more'
'Share things'
'Drawing great pictures'

The bottom right-hand has a red 'stop' traffic light showing and these are the things we want to change or get John to drop:

'Getting mad when I lose a game'
'Telling fibs'
'Forgetfulness'

Notice that we have stuck a picture of Mr. Forgetful (from 'Mistermen') in this quarter. This forgetful bit was partly in fun. It helped to lighten the atmosphere whilst still giving a message and helping John to discuss things.

Trees

In Chapter One I described how I had used this idea to serve two purposes with Jamie who had to wait several months before being able to move in-

120

FIG. 41

to his new family. I wanted him to be able to get the feel of time, and to have a visual image of the months going by and his getting nearer to the day he went to live with the Glovers, and I also wanted to monitor and discuss with him his behaviour and the interaction within the prospective foster family.

Figure 41 shows you the way this game was played. There were sections of time representing four months, September to December, and then a final section for 'living with my new family'. For each month Jamie had to wait I provided a cut-out tree which grew bigger by the month. At least the top grew bigger and we *hoped* the roots system would grow bigger.

But before pasting the new tree in to show how much Jamie had 'grown into' the family (because he was there at weekends and the half-term school holiday week) we had to discuss how things were going. We talked about how 'open' Jamie and his foster parents were. Did any of them say hurtful things or refuse to help or do other things which 'made the roots shrivel?'

You see, I'd explained that the tree was really Jamie (symbolic again) and there were lots of beetles around which ate the roots. We wanted to see Jamie's roots getting stronger and bigger. Sometimes because of what had happened I had to snip a bit of the root system off, but nevertheless it *did* get bigger and stronger each month until finally we pasted on a really strong looking tree 'A Tree called Jamie'. That was four years ago. Before I complete this book Jamie should be happily adopted.

Concluding Remarks.

In this chapter I have given a few more examples of the use of the *third object* ('games' or 'instruments') where there were certain objectives in view, and where I was to some extent focussing the discussion, although at the same time allowing the child to lead off in a different direction if he wished. This freedom of movement is also seen in Figure 16, the sociogram game when the child suddenly wanted to talk about dreams and 'things I don't like'. You will notice two stuck-on flaps we used for discussing those subjects.

I opened this chapter with some illustrations concerning ways of helping to discuss what I called *social and psychosocial* aspects. The work with Peter was used as an example. He was in that difficult two-way pull situation which involved interaction with, and feelings concerning, his foster parents and his natural mother and stepfather. Notice, however, that the instruments or third objects were also *(at the same time)* facilitating the clarification of his situation and planning of his future placement.

It was the same with Carl when I used the doll's house and the story of 'Mint' (the cat) to help in clarifying his psychosocial situation and interactions; at the same time Carl was involved in a planning role.

I also considered the use of the materials in situations where I felt there was a need to openly discuss the emotional reactions, although of course it must by now be clear to the reader that this aspect is likely to emerge at any point and when any objective is to the fore, be it *planning, behaviour-change* or whatever.

The last objective I considered in this chapter was *behaviour change* when, amongst other illustrations, we looked at the work with Jamie ('What is a Family') and also considered Fitzgerald's work with George in a residential setting.

Before moving on to Chapter Four in which we shall look at *regression-play* and the use of materials intended to stimulate sensory experience, it will be worthwhile pausing, again, to consider the way in which our materials may be used in a guiding, more *directed* manner, or in a complete-ly free and non-directed way. I referred to this in Chapter One, but so far I have described the use of materials in a more *focussed* manner, focuss-ing on particular areas which need clarification or, for examaple, some way of allowing the child to express feelings.

Non-directed play is vitally important and this will be seen in the work discussed in Chapter Four. Certainly, in undertaking therapy work with deprived and emotionally damaged children the emphasis, particularly in early stages of treatment, will be on the use of non-directed play (or other free forms of self-expression), but I am conscious of the fact that *most* of the children who are needing family placements, or who are being rehabilitated to their own families, or who have been adopted, are not in need of 'treatment' (e.g. psychotherapy) but are reasonably healthy kids who need to be able to talk and to get things sorted out. I am also aware that many adult workers find it difficult to get the child and themselves exchanging ideas on some of these delicate areas. The 'games' I have spoken about have helped these conversations along.

However, in Chapter Four I shall describe activities under the *nurture enrichment* section which I use to a much greater extent as free-play methods. But do bear in mind that many of the 'games' already described are also used for free-play. These could include things like dolls houses, toy cars, toy people, and of course the drawing, painting, modelling, cutting-out and sticking-on paraphernalia.

This book is intended for therapists and non-therapists. I want people to feel free in using *third objects* in the best way in their circumstances.

Having introduced the reader to a number of techniques and given some consideration to the objectives we may have in mind when working with children, I would like to draw attention to Appendix 'B' which sets out a check-list intended as a guide when preparing a child for long-term placement.

CHAPTER FOUR

Nurturing Enrichment, Regression-Play and Planning.

Much of the discussion about children who disrupt in the foster homes or within their own families tends to focus on the child's behaviour, that is to say his or her *social* behaviour. So we find ourselves and the caregivers wondering how best to cope with aggressive behaviour, or with withdrawn behaviour, or isolated acts such as 'telling lies' or 'stealing' and so forth.

However, some caregivers are troubled by the child's *backwardness*, or *messyness*, or *'refusal to learn'*, or his desire to play only with children much younger than himself. The caregivers tend to get worked up because of what people will think of the way they are bringing up the child. 'She's five but she still calls me to attend to her when she's been to the lavatory' or 'He's quite intelligent and is getting on alright at school but he still doesn't understand the idea of *time*. It makes me cross because I know he could understand it if he'd concentrate'.

What we need to understand is that children who have suffered deprivation, or the *trauma* of deprivation may, as a result, be less able to 'understand' ordinary experiences. They have missed out on babyhood and toddlerhood experiences to do with touching, hearing, seeing and even tasting.

"How come?" you may say. "They've always been able to *see* and they've been able to *feel*. Why do you say they've missed out?"

Well, for one thing their nurturing may have been very poor, or it could have been confusing being passed from one person to another, none of them adequate caregivers. What do I mean by nurture and nurturing? The ordinary dictionary definition of nurturing will probably go something like this:

'To provide, in the case of plants, animals, children and other living things, those conditions which are favourable to their healthy growth and development'.

If we take this last word 'development' and think about what this means for child-nurturing we shall see that it means an awful lot. Certainly food and warmth and shelter are part of nurturing, but if children are to develop into stable, understanding, life-enjoying and self-controlling adults they need far more than these material provisions, important though they are. For one thing parents and other caregivers must *talk* to infants, even to babies who will not understand words but who will nevertheless experience the communication. Later on they will link-up actual word-sounds with the experiences which come through sight or touch. They will themselves be able to use words meaning *red* or *green* or *yellow* when they experience those colours or, as we say, when they see those colours.

Good nurturing, as well as providing food, talk, love and affection will also supply thousands of opportunities to link the experiences of touch, sight, sound, smell, and taste to words and meaning. All these experiences are to do with the senses (those I've mentioned) and eventually with the child being able to develop *ideas* or concepts about the world around him such as space, distance, time, 'up', 'down', 'in', 'under', and so forth.

Many deprived children, that is to say children who have been deprived of a good nurturing experience, need to be given an opportunity to re-experience or to experience for the first time all sorts of enjoyable sensory stimulants. This may mean that we have to actually allow the child to 'be babyish' for a bit. We call this regression-play (or regressive-play). It doesn't mean that we want to keep him that way and the fact is, that provided he is enabled to experience some of these enjoyments of colour, sound, touch and so on, we are more likely to be successful in helping him to move on and do more 'advanced' things.

Sometimes these sensory experiences need to be linked into actual relationship or person-to-person situations. Because of this I have 'bottle-fed' children of five or six or older, actually holding them and feeding them with a baby's bottle. There are other, more ordinary, sensation experiences which children can enjoy, such as taking their shoes and socks off and running about on a lawn when the grass is wet.

Nurture Enrichment: Sensory Experience Activities.

One of the best and most delightful books describing sensory experience games is *Windows to our Children*, (Oaklander 1978) already referred to. One of the experiences Violet Oaklander describes is 'foot painting':

'Foot painting? Yes, foot painting! The feet are very sensitive, and they are mostly locked up in shoes where they can't feel anything. Lynn Pelsinger, a marriage, family, and child counsellor and special education teacher, uses foot painting with groups of children in special classes in the public schools. She will ask the children to take off their shoes and socks — not encouraged in school very often, unfortunately — and describe how their feet feel now that they are free. She tells them they will paint with their feet. After this idea sinks in she asks them to tell about what they can imagine their feet will be able to do. Then she places butcher paper on the floor and small trays of paint. She directs them to see how much paint they can get with their toes and what happens when the paint is released. The children will experiment with this for a while and then go on to painting with all parts of the feet, walking on the paper to make a variety of prints, painting with various toes, painting with the heel, the sides of the foot, trying each foot to notice any differences'.

Violet Oaklander has similar sensory experience activities for sight, sound, smell and taste. She describes the sensation value of working in wood, clay and even with 'junk'. "Some of the children did 'junk sculpture". On individual blocks of wood they nailed, glued, stapled, taped and nailed some more, until each had a fantastic original creation. We then sprayed the pieces with gold or silver paint and they shone as true works of art!!'"

In *nurture-enrichment* we aim to re-alert the senses.

Water Play.

Sinks, baths, or even small bowls of water can give children very real sensory learning experiences as well as fun. When young children empty the water from one jug or can into another; when they sink boats; or even if they use old washing-up liquid containers as water squirters, they are getting all sorts of sensations associated with touch and not only touch, but sight (reflections, colours in bubbles, etc.) and sounds. The child hears the sound of running water or dripping or splashing water.

I referred to *young* children doing these things, but we must remember that some much older children, even children of ten or eleven who have not experienced good nurturing, may need this form of play. Sometimes we may need to devise some form of water manipulation which doesn't look like *play*. This is because the older child who really wants to enjoy these sensations may be inhibited about what he sees as 'babyish'.

With young children of four, five or six years of age I have sometimes combined the watery experience with imagination games, using little plastic figures which float or 'swim' in the water. Some of the little family figures made by 'Galt Toys' will float. So I may start the water game off by making the figures speak and do things. Like this:

'Here you are, look. They're all going to have fun in the swimming pool. Here's the dad, he says "Come on children, jump in! Watch me"

......whoops! splash! "Oh, this is lovely".

'Now the little boy jumps in......splash! Down he goes and up he bobs again......look here's a little boat, we'll use this little tin as a boat......there you are, the dad is sitting in the boat......'

And so the story and the game develop.

Some children will take to this sort of play. Others simply want to squeeze things — sponges are useful — or float or even blow things into the water. Ann Hennessy of 'Project Children' in Birkenhead gave me a fun idea for water play. She lets the children put some 'bubble bath' liquid into the basin of water and then, with a piece of plastic tubing, the child can blow into the water and produce a mountain of bubbles.

Now bubbles are not just bubbles! They reflect all sorts of irridescent colour patterns. So then I may say:

Me: 'Look at that lovely blue colour in the bubbles — can you see other colours?'

Child: 'Yes......there's red......and green.....and I can see the window......I can see lots of windows in the bubbles'.

Me: 'Let's make them pop'.

The Great Outdoors.

Sensory enriching experiences need not and should not of course be confined to indoor activities. Children should be given 'natural' everyday experiences which go toward satisfying the need all humans have to relate in this way to physical objects and to experience phenomena.

The trouble is that grown-ups have forgotten the excitement of these ordinary experiences and they don't realise either that they are necessary for good all-round development, nor that they afford learning opportunities to children. Then we get the caregiver, who is more of a caretaker and wants to keep the child spotless, or puts her in the wrong clothes for enjoying sensory experiences:

'Get off that log dear, you'll dirty your dress......Oh, and don't walk in all that wet grass, I've told you before, you'll ruin your shoes'.

'No Peter, down off that tree......no tree climbing......trees are very dirty, besides you'll tear something. I know the other boys are climbing dear, but they're just rough lads'.

Rough, yes, and a damned sight more healthy probably.

Alexander, whom I introduced in Chapter Three and who displayed some strange neurotic behaviour, first presented to me as a hunched, crouching child of eleven years who would only glance, with a sideways glance, occasionally at the person addressing him. When I first took him walking in a small forest he hung back and said nothing. As we walked along I did some talking, 'to myself' it seemed. I said the names of the few trees I knew. I kicked the dried leaves about and kept pointing to colours and saying things about them.

Later in these rambles Alexander would run on ahead. He would scramble up fallen logs. He even displayed daring, which I encouraged by telling him he'd start getting known as daring by other kids at school. But now and again I'd get Alexander to stand still, or sit still, and I'd say:

"listen to all the sounds......see how many sounds we can hear".

Then we would notice sounds such as rustling leaves, or the rippling of a stream, maybe a tractor chugging away somewhere in the distance, birds, a human voice, and even, if we'd just run up some steep bank, the sounds of our hearts beating! (Perhaps we *felt* them more than heard them).

You remember Jamie — 'A Tree called Jamie'. He said he was scared to climb trees, so I went off into a nice woodland walk and we soon found nice climbable trees. But that wasn't all — we decided to build a woodland house or shelter. There were plenty of dried twigs and even small branchlets lying on the ground. We didn't need to be destructive. We were on the edge of the wood so there was also plenty of unused cut grass lying about in the meadow next to us.

Jamie hurried backwards and forwards with armfuls of grass, whilst I distributed it over the twigs supporting the roof. He had never had fun like this. But I knew that it wasn't just fun. Jamie was experiencing so much healthy sensory enjoyment.

I remember playing the same game with a little girl of about eight whose parents were fairly well-off and who lived in a large country house. This child had perfect (adult) manners and mannerisms. You could 'take her anywhere', but she had nevertheless missed the fun of childhood and the opportunities to really *experience* to the full the joy of sensory participation in the world about her.

Of course, large movement is to be encouraged. So all the bouncing and tumbling and rolling games and exercises are included as part of development.

Let Them Hear

We know now that sound should play a vital function in our nurturing experience. Babies of only a few weeks old apparently distinguish the voice of their mother (or other principal caregiver) and respond to the special sound of that voice. We know what a valuable experience can be had by mentally handicapped children, and even children said to be autistic, from a music experience. The music may be very simple or it may be highly complex. Different children will respond to different music.

In our modern western society we have, so to speak, shut our ears to sounds. Or perhaps we could say that the sounds are there but they have no meaning. Damaged children, the ones I have been talking about, are likely to have shut out certain sounds. I don't mean they can't hear them. It's rather like the tick of a clock. Sometimes you only notice the clock *has been* ticking away when it suddenly stops ticking because it wanted winding up. Mind you, we're fast doing away with ticking clocks altogether but you know what I mean.

The important thing in all this is to help children, those who have experienced deprivation, to get in touch with the world around them through sound.

With younger children, and even older children, you can play a guessing game. You ask the child or children to listen carefully and then tell you what the sound is. You make a sound which is very familiar, such as putting the lid on a teapot or stirring a teacup, and the child has to tell you what the sound is. Of course, the children love making the sounds as well for you to guess. I would avoid turning this into a competitive game. We get too much of that these days. If you turn them into competitive games the children concentrate on winning rather than on *experiencing*.

With music, recorded music, or instrumental if you are able to play an instrument, the child can be asked to listen for a while and then say what the sounds remind him or her of. Only short extracts need to be played, sometimes just a few bars, but these may conjure up storms, fairies, soldiers, waves in the sea, happy or sad memories and so on.

Sometimes I have combined a musical experience with acting. The child Wendy whom I've already written about, liked to have a melodramatic short play (very short, about six minutes) all worked out. She, or rather *we*, would then mime the whole thing to a piece of recorded 'classical' music. When making up the play the conversation would go something like this:

Wendy: "Pretend you go to a war and I get taken away and made into a slave".

Me: "Yes, alright, and then you get sold to a nasty owner".

Wendy: "And he beats me and I only get bread and water".

Me: "I know a piece of music which suddenly goes all sad just after a really loud, lively bit....then it suddenly livens up again. We'll do it to that".

And so the play would go on. Wendy would be taken prisoner and I would change from a charmer to a villian in a matter of a moments, pretending to thrash her (all in mime I hasten to say) then she would collapse to the floor and I'd retreat. There followed the 'sad' movement when she held the stage alone. Suddenly the music took off again and I would have to be the returning hero. I thrashed around with my sword while the music got wilder and finally the slave dealer succeeded to my skill. At that moment the music brought in the finale just as I rescued the maiden. Wendy loved performing this pantomime. It no doubt served more than one purpose, but the *sound*, the music, was all important as it expressed the feelings behind the mime.

Rudolph Dreikurs (1965) quoted by Oaklander says, when discussing the effects of music on psychotic children:

> Using music brought results in cases where other approaches had failed. It seems that the pleasant experience with music, often merely in the background, stimulates participation, permits an increase in the child's attention span, and raises his frustration tolerance. External and internal tensions disappear as reality becomes more pleasant and less threatening. The demands for participation are so subtle that they are not resented or defied'. (pp201-202).

Dreikurs mentions music as a background to other activity. This use of music, usually of a soothing kind, should be remembered because it can stimulate participation and is a pleasant sensory experience.

Thinking, Understanding, Knowing.

Sometimes I have met children who seemed to find it hard to grasp an idea and yet they would not have been considered as mentally handicapped within the normal meaning of that term. There was the case of Daniel, the seven year old, who just didn't seem to grasp the idea of time in terms of days, weeks and months. I spoke about him in Chapter One.

Daniel's foster parents were concerned because they felt it made the child look silly when he got all his days mixed up, and after carefully learning parrot-fashion the days of the week in their correct order would tell you in the next breath that because today is Tuesday, tomorrow will be Sunday! Or would tell you on Wednesday that 'next week is tomorrow'.

I felt he needed to 'see' and 'feel' time in a way that would make it easier for him to grasp the idea. So I devised a game (see Figure 42) on a board divided into days and weeks. For each day there was a square about 6 x 6 cmts. Every day, in the appropriate square, Daniel drew a picture of the weather as you will see in my illustration. I had provided a set of simple drawings to be copied or traced. So he drew a blazing sun with rays streaming out if the day was bright with sunshine; a windmill if it was a very windy day, and so on. This helped to give him a feeling about that day.

As well as drawing in the weather, Daniel had to move a little cardboard figure representing himself. This meant that he could see himself moving across the week and eventually across the whole month. After about six weeks he was able to cope well with the idea of days and weeks, and he enjoyed putting in the symbols. He did some of them in colour — that was his own idea. I've used this learning method with other children since helping Daniel.

FIG. 42

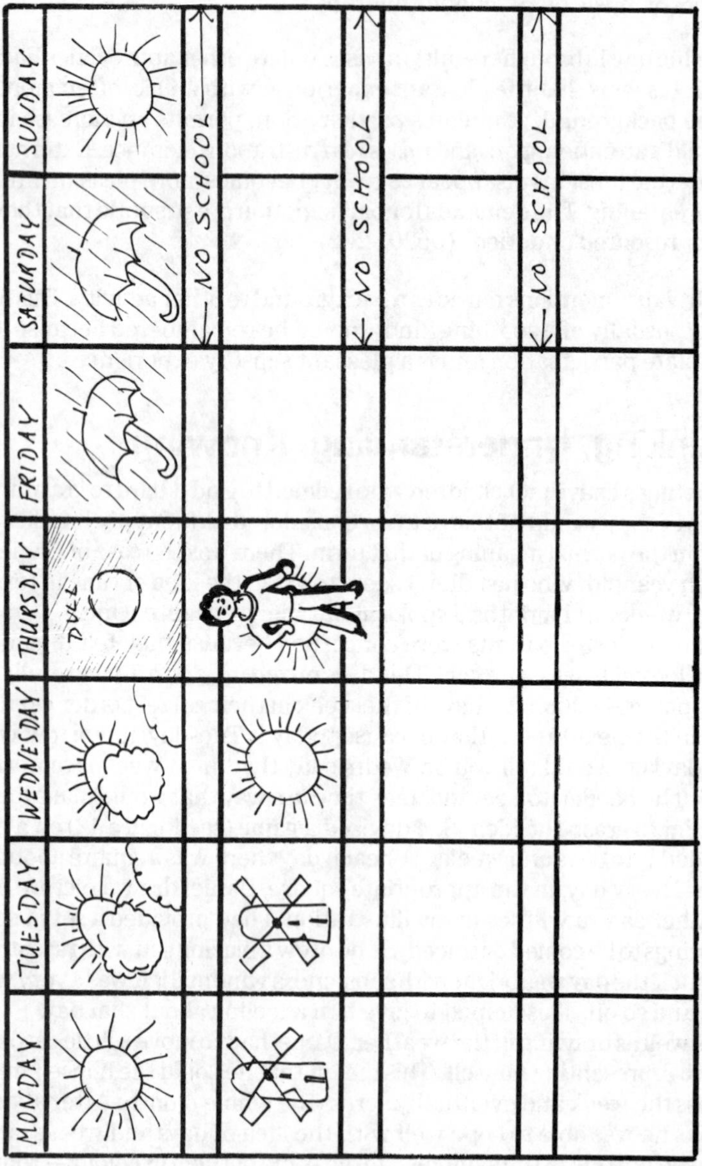
MONDAY
TUESDAY
WEDNESDAY
THURSDAY
FRIDAY
SATURDAY
SUNDAY
DULL
NO SCHOOL
NO SCHOOL
NO SCHOOL

TIME Chart, the figure is moved each day and the weather symbol drawn in

If I may use a few technical words here it will help those who are not so familiar with the jargon when they come across the terms in further reading. This *grasp* of ideas is often referred to as concept forming or *conceptualising*. Generally speaking, as the child grows and develops, he is able to conceive of more complex ideas. Children who have experienced emotional and social deprivation may have difficulty in conceptualising. This difficulty may show up over concepts associated with time as in Daniel's case, or with space (including distance) and shape.

Concept forming is part of what psychologists call the *cognitive* aspects of mental function. That is to say the 'knowing' part of our experience (as distinct from our emotional experiences). Cognition includes judging, reasoning, remembering, imagining and perceiving as well as concept-forming. Jeanette McCollum (1984) writes:

'Social Interaction between infant and caregiver is not only a source of mutual pleasure, it is also perhaps the major setting in which the infant practises and learns social, *cognitive and* communication skills' (my italics).

More and more we are coming to understand how the whole child may be affected, or various aspects of personality and body function may be affected, by depriving the child not necessarily of food or clothing, but of affection, conversation, cuddling and playing with. So many of the children I have tried to help have experienced poor parenting at some time in their lives where the *interaction* between child and caregiver was poor. Terence Gaussen (1984) writes:

'Thus cognitive and social development, together with early language and communication, are now being described as part of one interdependent process in interaction with caregivers....and in some instances early social relationships may affect even motor development quite radically'.

By 'motor development' is meant the ability to use limbs, muscles, fingers, etc. in movement and manipulation.

I have met foster parents who felt really frustrated because their foster children of six or seven years of age could not, or 'would not', learn to dress themselves or tie their shoe laces. Having gone into it in some detail with the caregivers and eliminated the possibility that the child was behaving in this way as an attention-seeking device, it often became clear that they had not developed the skill to co-ordinate their motor (muscular, fingers, arms, legs) functions with their space, shape concepts, so things got pulled in the wrong direction. Some mothers wanted their children to take their jumpers off by that arms-crossing motion where they then grab the hem of the garment and swing it over their heads. It's hard for us to realise how complicated such a 'simple' movement is in terms of all the messages to and from the brain, and all the previous 'programming' required to learn that function.

Sensory experiences, then, are vital for proper development. But along with one kind of sensory experience such as sight or, to be more specific, *colour,* the growing child has to have other sensory experiences of sound, or *words,* in order to associate a particular word with a particular colour. The child must experience movement, shape, distance, and all sorts of tactile (touch) experiences in order to be able to conceptualise, to *think,* to understand. It may be necessary to provide sensory experiences where the child has suffered nurturing deprivation.

Some older children need a regressive form of play. That is to say they need to play games which much younger children would normally play, or to use materials associated with young children. They probably wouldn't be seen indulging in such play usually, and certainly not with their own peer group, for fear of being called 'baby' or thought of as being odd or 'thick'. They need to be able to play, perhaps with sand, water or clay, in the privacy of their own home or in some other place where even their own siblings can't make fun of them. They may need sensory experiences associated with early nurturing, such as bottle-feeding.

There are materials such as clay and wood, and even those produced at a half-way stage in the cookery process — pastry dough, for example — which can be used to give older children tactile and other sensory experiences without their seeming 'babyish'. These are experienced sometimes in the school routine in 'cookery' or 'woodwork', etc., but they need to be experienced and enjoyed in a very free routine and without the pressure of the classroom or the fear of not doing as well as other children. Teenagers, and even adults, like to 'doodle' in materials as well as 'doing it properly'. Eventually, of course, 'doing it properly' could bring the added satisfaction of having created something as well as the satisfaction derived from the basic sensory experiences, but some teenagers do need to regress with the materials.

Self-healing and sensory-descriptive materials.

The very opposite to the use of the games, instruments and materials for *focussing* or directing conversation, is the free-choice use of these things and where the therapist, for now I am talking more of therapy, does not direct the 'play' at all. The various sensory and descriptive-imaginative pieces of equipment I have described so far in this chapter lend themselves to this use.

What is more often than not overlooked is that unresolved conflicts and the essential 'replay' of impressionable events may be handled by the child as she 'plays' with certain pieces of equipment.

I can think of one child who 'replayed' funerals using a lot of little models (or 'toys') and making some of the required things himself. This child was not requiring psychotherapeutic treatment but it would seem that he needed to enact the funeral scenes in which he had been recently involved, in real life. So, little cardboard boxes were gently placed inside tiny model cars and tiny cardboard wreaths and sprays of flowers were cut out, coloured, and placed on the grave. This was all done with dolls-house size toys.

It is helpful to have whole villages which may be used for constructing 'scenes' and enacting events. These 'villages' need only to be comprised of small articles, and the fact that the various articles are not to scale doesn't matter all that much. I have little houses that are made from blocks of wood (the people can't go inside them except in the child's imagination). They stand about six or seven centimetres in height. Then there are cars, buses, road signs, fences, farm animals, wild beasts, soldiers, spacemen, trees, lavatory basins (often called upon) and so on and so forth. All sorts of scenes are enacted by the children in free-play.

I do not intend to go into the various hypotheses or theories which lie behind the use of much of this material or which account for the curative effect such play seems to have on many children. Readers will find certain books on Play-Therapy named in my further reading list. It is important, however, that the self-healing value of free-play using free-choice of materials (sand, clay, paints, felt pens, water, dolls houses, models, etc), should be appreciated.

Some of the theories concerning the use of these materials for psychotherapy are highly developed, sometimes controversial, and beyond the scope of this book. Some therapists will ask the child to describe what the scene is about, or what the picture represents, and there is little doubt that such a procedure helps the child to 'own' or 'accept' certain symbolic expressions which emerge in the course of using the materials. Lowenfeld's (1979) sand-tray work (or play) has seen a revival recently. In her therapy she used the sand-tray with the sort of models I've described concerning 'villages', but the actual sand itself has meaning and is used by the child for dealing with real-life stresses both at a pre-conscious and unconscious level (although Lowenfeld would say *pre-verbal* rather than *unconscious*). She observed that some children, when using the sand-tray method, were able eventually to gain control over powerful internal and destructive aggressive impulses. Her work of course was highly professional and the method should be used only by those who have received training in it.

However, I am concentrating on the implicit value and self-healing properties that *sensory, imaginative* and creative activity of this sort has for damaged children. These materials may be used by therapist and non-therapist — in fact by 'good-enough' parents. But the materials used in this way are used by me in a non-directed, or as I prefer to say, a *non-focussed* (free-play) manner.

In the following section on *planning* I revert to the more heavily focussed use of materials. At the stage where planning is being undertaken openly with a child, my assumption is that either the child has already been helped by the use of non-focussed free-play or that this is not a child requiring that treatment.

PLANNING TOGETHER.

This book is about working with children. Partly, however, it is aimed at helping the child and the adult to obtain a better picture of the events in the child's life and to help him or her to come to terms with those past events. I have also touched on work which has the main objective of giving the child an opportunity to explore the environment and gain pleasurable and useful sensory experiences.

Now I would like to look rather more specifically at work (or play) which is aimed at involving the child in planning for the future. Before actual planning starts a good deal of direct work should have been done with the child in order for both child and worker to understand the past and the present situation in which the child finds herself. It is no good planning to rehabilitate the child into her natural family if the court that took her out of it and made her a Ward has not already agreed to such a plan. Equally, it is no good planning an adoption placement with the child if the likelihood is that the natural parents will be given the care of the child before very long.

Readers will find references to planning with children in several of the books given in my further reading list. Fitzgerald refers to this aspect of the work (1982). In the chapter 'Planning for Family Placement' he briefly mentions a number of children, and says of Martin:

> 'Martin, aged seven, who previously had been placed with a couple who had a child of their own and were unable to provide the stimulation that he needed, was also able to ask John Fitzgerald for a new Mum and Dad, stipulating that "They must be interesting, they must like me, and I don't want any other children". In this way he had captured the sadness of his previous situation'.

Vera Fahlberg (1981) also has advice, some of it very practical, for when children are moving into a placement. Here she is talking about work with a *verbal* child who is moving from a short-term placement into an adoptive placement:

> 'Following the second visit the social worker can talk separately with the prospective adoptive family, the child, and the foster family. The social worker needs to get everyone's opinions about how things are go-

ing, so that he can decide whether to plan to move the child into the family. When the worker has this information at hand and finds it favourable, he should get the child and the adoptive parents together and ask each in front of the other, already knowing the answers, if they want to proceed with the move. Then the plan for a further visiting schedule and the final move can be outlined'.

Despite the fact that Fahlberg's procedure as outlined here is necessarily neat and clipped (e.g. making a final decision after two visits) and does not include safeguards such as 'Adoption Panels', the text does emphasise the planning as going on *with the child's involvement*, which is what I wanted to bring out.

Group work with older children is possible, and Phillida Sawbridge (1983) gives an account of such work with a group of mentally handicapped children:

'It had been agreed previously that, in order to have a degree of stillness and concentration for work, the children would first need to use up some of their energy so the first game was shipwreck, which we played twice. Then followed a treasure hunt consisting of a set of six postcards of pop stars which had been prepared in the individual colours of the badges (i.e. badges worn by social worker group leaders). Although obvious hiding places had been chosen, some of the group had great difficulty in finding them and in identifying the different colours..... Throughout all this time Sonia had either been out in the hall or had stood apart, resisting all attempts to bring her into the group.

At this point, 'formal' work began with the *Parents for Children* co-ordinator explaining why we were all there, i.e. to explore different possibilities for the future. A large piece of paper was fixed to the wall, and with the help of the group we listed all the things they had in common, e.g. all in care, living in children's homes, or going to special schools, etc. Some of the group were reluctant to accept that they were at a special school. During this session Sonia sat away from the group but half turned towards them, not participating but listening to everything that we said.

Then we explored what the children liked or disliked about living in a children's home and how they would expect it to be different in a family'.

In the book 'Opening New Doors', Kay Donley (1975) writes:

'Someone asked me if we give the child the record on the family to read! I must confess I have not, but maybe that is not a bad idea. I know that most of the workers use the same kinds of materials that go into adoption study documents to explain to the child the kind of family this is, but we have found that this is too complicated for most kids and so we

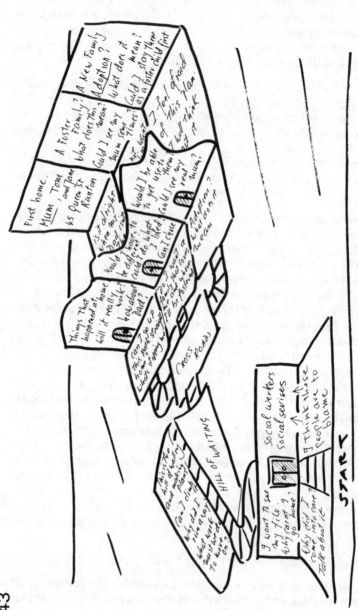

FIG. 43

try to use descriptions and photographs of the family, their house and animals. Animals are extremely important to most children and lots of our families seem to keep pets, but even as you go into introductions the child who is available for adoption is still given to understand that this is not an adoption home, this is a possibility of a family for him. We have got to be very square about that, that not all such introductions do in fact culminate in placement'.

Many of the games I have already discussed will be of use in planning with children. I will refer back to some of those a little further on. Now I'd like to look at some ideas I've used, especially when working with children and helping them to participate in making plans for their future. As with many of the ideas already discussed, these planning games may extend over a period of weeks if not months.

One such game, which I call 'The Marathon Walk', developed from a little rough sketch made in a child's exercise book. The basic idea was to show the child that he could move forward towards a goal, even though when the game started we did not know what the end goal would be. The child I first played Marathon Walk with had one goal in mind, to return to his natural mother. I represented the forward planning as a road leading to his natural mother, but then I drew some large 'road blocks' which might be temporary hindrances but might even represent a permanent blockage in that direction. One of the road blocks, perhaps only a hindrance, was the fact that his mother had no home of her own.

In this game I usually make the roadway with sections, as you find in a game such as 'Ludo', and we then represent the child with a counter and move him or her along as the game proceeds. This means that the youngster I've mentioned above moved up until he got to the road block 'Mother has no house' and then he had to wait there whilst we discussed the reality of this situation. In fact, in his case this housing problem could have become something more than a hindrance because his mother had been evicted several times and owed hundreds of pounds to more than one housing authority.

Figure 43 shows a development of this game designed for a child who at the start of the game was living resentfully in a children's home. She had a lot of anger directed towards social workers, both field and residential. She was a persistent absconder who had twice been fostered. At home with her natural parents her behaviour was, if anything, worse. But underneath all that was a sad, wounded young soul seeking security but not ready to trust anyone.

You will see from Figure 43 that I made walls going right across the board. Only when we (the child and I) had reached a stage when the discussion could move forward would we take the scissors and cut open one of the doors so as to let the child through for further discussion.

FIG. 44

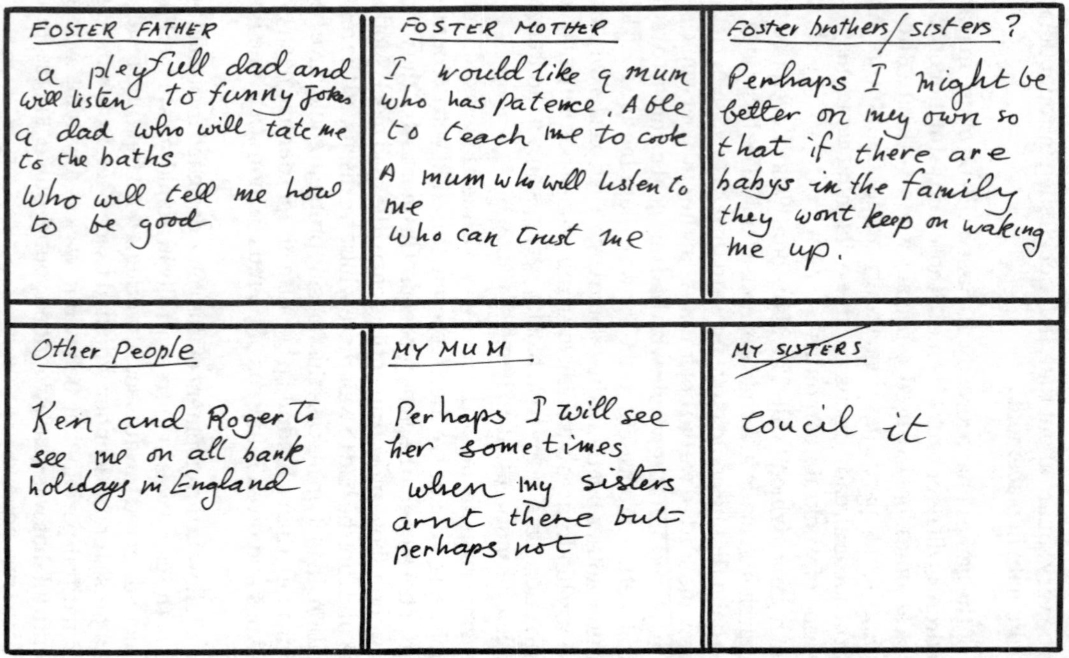

FOSTER FATHER	FOSTER MOTHER	Foster brothers/sisters?
a playfull dad and will listen to funny jokes a dad who will take me to the baths Who will tell me how to be good	I would like a mum who has patience, Able to teach me to cook A mum who will listen to me Who can trust me	Perhaps I might be better on my own so that if there are babys in the family they wont keep on waking me up.
Other People	MY MUM	MY SISTERS
Ken and Roger to see me on all bank holidays in England	Perhaps I will see her some times when my sisters arnt there but perhaps not	couldn't it

Some of Jamie's ideas about foster parents and his natural family

In the first section we had to deal with why the child came into care. We also had to look at her anger and to think about her views on who was to 'blame' (her word) for her not being allowed home immediately.

The time came when the door could be opened, but then she had a hill to climb. The hill was called 'The Hill of Waiting and Planning'. Down the side of the road leading up the hill we wrote things about how she felt and questions she wanted dealt with. We had things like 'What is there to talk about?', 'Is my own behaviour making it hard to plan?', 'Have I got any say in what happens?', 'Will people listen to me?', 'What work must we do to move on?'

When she had worked her way over the hill and was at least calm enough to talk about alternatives, it meant she'd reached the 'crossroads' which you will see in Figure 43. She might still choose to go left towards the door leading to her first home and her mum, so the counter would move in that direction. Here it might sit for a long time because I would only allow the door to open leading to that plan if it was practical and the child was ready to risk another trial, and of course the social services' panel (responsible for the care of the child) was in agreement. Furthermore, I would have to be satisfied that the parents were able to make some adjustments otherwise we'd simply land back at 'start' in three months' time.

So the door may or may not be opened. Planning *with* the child must not be mistaken for planning *by* the child. So far as is possible I like to go with the child and sustain her and the caregivers whoever they may be, but it is equally important that she should be helped to cope with the frustration resulting from avenues which are unrealistic or blocked.

If the 'rehabilitation to own family' door cannot realistically be opened (perhaps just at that time) then, depending on various factors, the child will be helped along another avenue. In the case I am describing we did eventually open the middle door. Our discussions and planning led to a fostering placement with foster parents who were well able to work with the child's natural parents.

You will see that in Figure 43, just beyond the door leading to fostering, the child wrote down such questions as 'Could I see my mum sometimes?', 'I would not want little kids there', i.e. other younger children in the foster home. So you see we were planning together even though, as in the lives of most of us, her immediate wishes are not always met. But in the end she found the understanding, affection, and patience she needed from caregivers who will, if she still wants it, help her to return to the companionship of her mother when she is a young adult.

But you don't need always to use such a complicated board game. I remember that when I was working with Jamie the time came when the reviewing team decided that we should advertise especially for permanent caregivers (possible adopters) for him. By this time Jamie had already expressed a very firm view requesting me to find a new family for him. So

FIG. 45

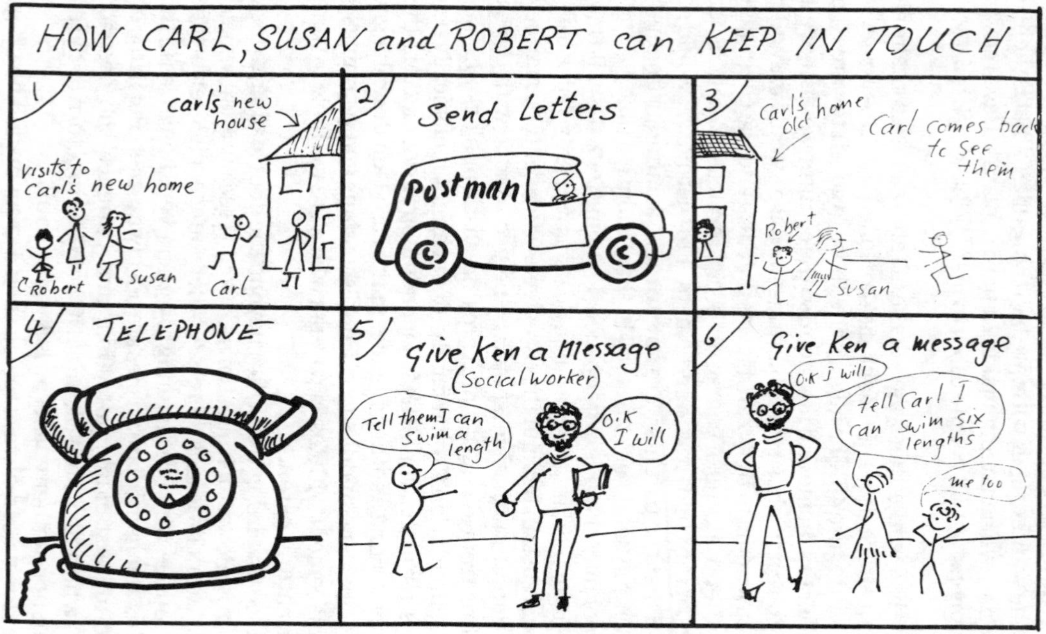

HOW CARL, SUSAN and ROBERT can KEEP IN TOUCH

we worked on the wording of the advertisement. Before actually doing the wording I felt it would be helpful if we could look at the sort of family we might be wanting to find. In order to have something to act slightly as a third object, I divided some sheets of typing paper into sections, see Figure 44, with headings under which we could put Jamie's ideas.

So, as you see, we had one section for 'Dad' and one for 'Mum'. Then there was one for 'Other Children in the Family'. Readers may wonder why the only words to be found under 'My Sisters' are 'council it'. The reason is that Jamie did not wish to involve them in any way with his plan for a new family. He felt this section was superfluous and so, taking the pen from my hand, he wrote in those words. In fact of course he should have spelt the message 'cancel it'!

With Carl (see Chapter Three) who required a nurturing experience impossible within his sibling group and who was very difficult for some people to handle, including teachers, I decided to let him see the sort of form I had got to complete concerning him. This form was called the 'homefinder' and it described the child in great detail and the sort of family he needed. Of course it didn't mean much to Carl. It was just that I knew it could take me some weeks to find the right family and I needed to help him understand what our task was. Having let him see the impressive form with all those little printed questions I was then able to produce a specially designed one which had simple headings and big spaces below for us to write in. In this, week by week, we tried to spell out what people should know about him. Some headings were:

> What Carl looks like.
> What Carl likes doing.
> What Carl likes to eat.
> How Carl has made people happy.
> How Carl has made people cross with him.

This gave him a feeling that he was involved with what was being said about him. It was just as important that Carl should, in due course, have information about the family I felt I'd found for him, and this was done.

Naturally, although Carl was able to accept the idea of a move to a new family, he was apprehensive since he was moving into the unknown and would be separated from his older sister and younger brother. So he'd need assurance, as part of the planning, that contact would be maintained with his siblings and his present caregivers. In order to let him see how communication could be maintained we drew some little pictures showing ways of keeping in touch. See Figure 45.

Planning: Using games we've used before.

Nearly all the games and equipment I have spoken of in previous chapters

FIG. 46

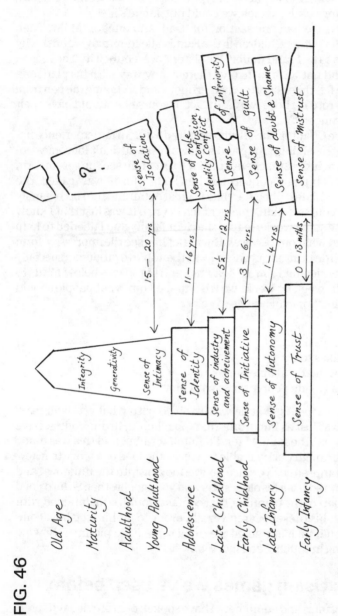

Diagram based on Erikson's crucial development tasks

may be used as part of plan-making when doing direct work with children.

If you think of the flow-chart idea, for example, it is easy to imagine how it can be applied to planning. The child and adult worker can project the chart forward and continue on from the present placement to a possible future placement. Instead of looking at what has happened the child would be encouraged to think about what she wants to see happening.

The sliders and sets of discussion cards can also be used when making plans. But now we would encourage the child to talk about how the people and objects or likes and dislikes named on the sliders would fit into the plans. So we'd find subjects such as 'my grandparents' and 'new school' appearing in the sets.

Another piece of equipment which certainly lends itself to planning is the board game I have described in Chapter Three (Figure 34). This is the game which shows the child how certain important factors in his life are fixed whilst others can change. I have used the game to help children learn about the transfer of responsibilities from the social care agency to future adopters. These are terribly important and often frightening things for children to cope with. We often fail to realise what it must feel like to know that a social care agency or a court holds tremendous power over your life, movements, and future. Or it may be the other way round; some children are apprehensive about what could happen if they became legally adopted. That board game can be very helpful.

Usually, when I'm doing this direct work with children, I find that we are not making just one use of the particular game but many. A clear instance of this is seen in the examples I gave for the work with Peter in Chapter Three. This was the child who was being pulled in two directions, either return to the care of his natural mother or stay with the foster family. You will remember that I drew up a series of possible placements using a system of drawing rings around the families. In Chapter Three I have put those illustrations under the heading *Clarifying Social and Psycho-social Aspects* (see Figures 22a, 22b and others). But the illustrations would have fitted just as well into the present section on planning, for that was just what Peter and I were doing, but the ring game also made it easier both to conceptualise around and to talk about the various possibilities. There is obviously an infinity of variations in the way we can help children to look into the future and to convey their thoughts to us. We must keep adjusting the games and even adjusting our style of talking, and we must use every particle of imagination in our direct work. And so of course play-acting (or role-play) can be used in planning, so can story writing and dolls house play. In fact almost any of the games I've spoken about, even those which were mainly employed for sensory experience, may be used for planning.

Conclusion.

In this chapter I introduced readers to games and ideas which will be useful when helping children to explore and enjoy sensory experiences. We looked briefly at the importance of such experiences as part of child development needs. In the latter part of the chapter we had a look at direct work where one is involved in planning the future for children who have not got a settled and satisfactory family placement already.

In all the work we do with children we must be very aware of what Thom (1984) calls 'misguided intervention'. I have already referred to the inappropriate use, or wrong timing, of certain techniques but it is also possible to do harm by an inappropriate *approach*. For example, although children need encouragement and will benefit from a right measure of praise or appreciation (for *effort* as well as result), this can be overdone so that it becomes unreal or even dishonest. If a child has a poor self-image 'all-embracing praise', says Thom, will not be believed and so will reinforce the poor self-image.

Another common form of 'misguided intervention' ('misguided' in therapy terms, that is) is starting too early with work directed at observable relationship problems, when the behaviour which the adults want to change is part of the child's method of self-preservation. The child who is emotionally *withdrawn* for example may tend to sit up in her own room. Simply talking about this, or even using the special techniques shown in this book, will not help her to cope with her inner problems. Something else needs to happen first.

I have tried to indicate how careful, and sensitive and aware we need to be if we are providing a service centred on children who have experienced deprivation. We are often dealing with very immature psyches; with children who may feel dreadfully threatened deep, deep down inside themselves, or even with children who cannot form, or understand, time-space concepts, or cause and effect, and with children who are forced to test-out aspects of life they should be taking for granted. Although we come to the work with pleasure and freshness, we should not take it lightly or thoughtlessly because we may do damage when we seek to mend.

Does it always work

I am aware that I have stressed the value and, as I have experienced it, the helpfulness of ideas and methods I have written about. I would not wish the reader, because of this, to be left with the notion that what I am promoting is some sort of panacea or some easy-method (guaranteed success) package. Sometimes the methods described here seemed to me to represent 'fruit-bearing' approaches whilst at other times, with other children, I might have ascribed more 'fruit-bearing' to other factors. Certainly there were children who spurned some of the methods whilst embracing others. I imagine, also, that much depends upon the particular worker and how he or she relates to children and young adults.

Finally, let me stress the importance of the caregivers being properly prepared and supported. Before a deprived child is placed with foster parents or adopters, those caregivers should have had the advantage of preparation and training. This is too large a subject to be covered here, but I make it my parting plea.

All that is written in this book is aimed at enabling children and adults to grow together (to fuse together) in an experience of affection, toleration and understanding. Diane, aged twelve, put it nicely to me when she intertwined the fingers of her hands as if about to pray and said, 'I want to join up with someone, like this'

FURTHER READING

Direct Work, Communication Techniques, Play Therapy.

'The Foster Child - Identity and the Life Story Book' by Anne-Marie Jones. Publisher: University College of North Wales.
This is a booklet published in type-script and therefore inexpensive. Very well written and thorough. Reviews several fostering models and includes a good discussion on the use of the Life Story Book method of helping children to achieve self-knowledge and a sense of identity.

'Working with Young Children: Encouraging their Development and Dealing with Problems' by J. Laishley. Publisher: Edward Arnold, 1983.
This practical book for foster parents, nursery staff, social workers and others describes how adults can be more active participants in children's pre-school development. Combines observation techniques, theory and practice.

'Art Therapy' at the Familymakers Project' by Ann Gillespie.
In journal, *Adoption and Fostering,* Vol.10, No. 1, 1986. Publisher: British Agencies for Adoption and Fostering (BAAF).
A helpful, brief, practical article with two short case studies and three illustrations of drawings.

'Bruce's Story' by Maureen Thom. Publisher: The Children's Society, London, 1986.
This is a story for children. It is about a dog, Bruce, but its aim is to help children, who have experienced changes and loss in their lives, to acknowledge and share their feelings. A good working tool.

'Play Therapy' by Virginia Axline. Publisher: Houghton Mifflin Co., Cambridge, Mass. 1947.
A very sensitive and important book. It gives eight guiding principles. It describes the application of 'non-directed' play and counselling based on Rogerian principles.

'Let Me Play' by Jeffree et al. Publisher: Souvenir Press (Human Horizons Series) 1977.
A very practical book describing dozens of games and activities designed for children from babyhood to school age. Suitable for parents and people looking after children in groups. Not a technical book but it does provide some easily understood theory of play.

'We Go Exploring' by Kargaard and Ekberg. Publisher: Lion Publishing. A book to use with young children. It is designed to help them in sensory experience and has materials to feel and to smell.

'Communicating Through Play' by Pat Curtis, in journal *Adoption and Fostering*. Vol. 6, No. 1, 1982. Publisher: British Agencies for Adoption and Fostering (BAAF).
A useful, short, introductory article of four pages length. Pat Curtis writes for residential care staff, foster parents and others.

'Use of the Geneogram with Adoptive Families' by Finch and Jaques, in journal *Adoption and Fostering*, Vol. 9, No. 3, 1985. Publisher: British Agencies for Adoption and Fostering (BAAF).
This article describes a technique which is also helpful for work with individual children, adopted, fostered or otherwise placed.

Social Work (Children) Practice.

'Working with Children' (Practice Papers). Publisher: British Agencies for Adoption and Fostering (BAAF) 1986.
An excellent book. A set of papers originally published as part of BAAF 'In Touch with Children' training pack. Covers child development, attachment theory, the social worker as a bridge, charts showing developmental progress, and the use of free play.

'Helping Children When They Must Move' by Vera Fahlberg. Publisher: British Agencies for Adoption and Fostering (BAAF) 1979.
A useful book for social workers and students. Provides a theory base, work sheets and case examples.

'Good Enough Parenting' by Adcock and White. Publisher: British Agencies for Adoption and Fostering (BAAF) 1985.
Blends theory and practice in a helpful way. Valuable to all child care workers and students.

'The Permanency Principle in Child Care Social Work' (Social Work Monographs, Monograph No. 21) by Catriona Morris. Publisher: University of East Anglia, Norwich, Norfolk, 1984/1985.
This is a helpful review of social work applied to long-term child care placements (adoption and fostering). It examines the value of direct work and preparation of the child for placement.

'Making Decisions About Children' by H.R. Schaffer in journal, *Adoption and Fostering*, Vol. 9, No. 1, 1985.
A useful seven page article. Not too technical but dealing with important issues of separation and deprivation in childhood. Touches on attachment and bonding and the reversibility of traumatic effects. Provides references for more extensive reading including books by the same author.

'Working with Children: The Violet Oaklander Approach' by M. Thom in journal, *Adoption and Fostering*, Vol. 8, No. 3, 1984. Publisher: British Agencies for Adoption and Fostering (BAAF).
A short but sensitive article. Very helpful and vital to all persons concerned with direct work with children.

'Identity and Security' by J. Triseliotis in journal, *Adoption and Fostering*, Vol. 7, No. 1, 1983. Publisher: British Agencies for Fostering and Adoption (BAAF).
An excellent short article with theory applicable to the theme of this book.

NOTE: The following three books are more extensive, in-depth studies suitable for social workers and social work students.

'In Search of Origins' by J. Triseliotis. Publisher: Routledge and Kegan Paul, 1973.

'Adoption: A Second Chance' by B. Tizard. Publisher: Open Books, London, 1977,

'Adopting Older Children' by A. Kadushin. Publisher: Columbia University Press, 1970.

Caregiver Practice.

'Children in Care Revisited' by Pamela Mann. Publisher: British Agencies for Adoption and Fostering (BAAF) 1986.
This is a casebook of biographies. It provides examples of good practice and shows perceptive insight on the part of the author.

'Adoption -The Inside Story', Edit. Judy Austin. Publisher: Barn Owl Books, 1986.
A helpful and revealing collection of articles by adoptive families, but just as helpful to foster parents and others concerned with child care.

'Helping Children to Cope with Separation and Loss' by Claudia Jewett. Publisher: British Agencies for Adoption and Fostering (BAAF) 1986.
Easy to understand. Helpful to parents and foster parents, residential staff and social workers.

'The Hyperactive Child: A Parent's Guide' by Eric Tayor. Publisher: Martin Dunitz, London, 1985.
A difficult subject dealt with in an easy to understand style. Suitable for all caregivers both lay and professional.

'Black Identity' (Workbook One) (Black Like Me Series) by J.E. Maxime. Publisher: Emani Publications, Beckenham, Kent, 1986.
This workbook is aimed at helping the child to achieve a positive black identity. Guidance notes for adults.

'Black Pioneers' (Workbook Two) (Black Like Me Series) by J.E. Maxime. Publisher: Emani Publications, Beckenham, Kent, 1986.
This workbook shows how black people have made, and continue to make, a vital contribution to the culture of the human race. Guidance notes for adults.

Popular-Descriptive Books.

'How Not to be a Perfect Mother' by Libby Purves. Publisher: Fontana Books.
Written in a chatty, witty style. It explains how to be a 'good enough' parent. Ideal for all caregivers.

'How it Feels to be Adopted' by Jill Krementz. Publisher: Gollancz, 1985
The book is directed at helping adopted children to realise that their own experiences, questions, frustrations, etc., are shared by others and are 'normal'.

Child Development, Behaviour and Psychology.

'Attachment and Separation' by V. Fahlberg. Publisher: British Agencies for Adoption and Fostering (BAAF) 1982.
This small, easy to follow book, by a leading practitioner in our subject, deals with attachment, assessing attachment, and separation. It provides check lists and exercises.

'Child Development' by V. Fahlberg. Publisher: British Agencies for Adoption and Fostering (BAAF) 1982.
A very useful, easy to understand book by a writer totally in tune with our subject. It is a good basic introduction to child development from birth to adolescence, and provides work sheets and exercises.

'The Needs of Children' by M. Kellmer Pringle. Publisher: Hutchinson & Co., London, 1975 (Reprints 1984).
Easy to follow. A good introduction to the basic needs for satisfactory child development.

NOTE: The following books are more extensive, in-depth studies suitable for social workers and social work students.

'Helping Troubled Children' by M. Rutter. Publisher: Penguin Books, 1975.

'Maternal Separation Re-assessed' by M. Rutter. Publisher: Penguin Books, 1972.

'Clinical Studies in Infant Mental Health' by S.H. Fraiberg. Publisher: Tavistock, London.

'Attachment and Loss' Vols. I, II and III by J. Bowlby. Publisher: Hogarth Press (1969), also Karnac Books, London, Penguin Books (Paperback) 1986.

'Touching: The Human Significance of the Skin' by A. Montague. Publisher: Columbia University Press 1971.
A very sensitively written book describing the biological and psychological importance of the sense of touch and the need to be touched.

'The Betrayal of the Body' by Alexander Lowen. Publisher: Collier Books and Macmillan Publishing Co., 1967.
Written by a medical doctor who has found (to quote from the blurb) 'that many people have actually denied the reality, needs and feelings of their own bodies'. The aim of his treatment is to achieve a 'gratifying mind-body relationship'.

APPENDIX A

The Story of David, Peter, and Alison

Although this story is told using basic English and simple sentences, it is quite complicated and includes 'in-care' placements and events which do not make it an account of good social work practice. But it resembles many real-life stories of children I have worked with.

It is an unfinished story because I have imagined that I have written it for the children soon after being engaged to undertake direct work with them, and to assess their future long-term needs. So it is intentionally open-ended and unfinished and intended to be added to. This story shows the children continuing to move from placement to placement even when received into care. What will be their future?

THE STORY OF DAVID, PETER, AND ALISON.

Once upon a time there was a very pretty young lady called Marlene. She had red hair which was long and went down over her shoulders. Marlene had lots of brothers and sisters.

One day Marlene, who liked dancing and singing and cooking, met a young man who fell in love with her. He was called Mr. Bright. So they got married. Here they are getting married.

Then one day Marlene had a little baby boy. She wondered what to call him. She knew her dad came from Wales, so she thought of a nice Welsh sounding name. She called him Owen.

Baby Owen in his cot

They all lived together and were happy at first. But sometimes grown-ups find things are not working out. It is sad if this happens, but sometimes it does happen. So Mr. Bright and Marlene had to go away from each other. Marlene and Owen stayed together and Owen grew up and went to school when he was five. Here is Owen and Marlene, his mum, going to the school.

One day Marlene, who was pretty and very kind, met another boy friend. He was called Roy. They liked each other and Roy said, 'Will you marry me?' So Marlene married Roy. Then there were three people in the family.

Roy   Marlen   Owen

But soon Marlene and Roy had a baby. He was a smashing baby. They called him David. So now there were four of them. Here they are:-

Dad   Mum   Owen   David

A bit later they had another super baby. This time Marlene chose another name from the Bible. They called him Peter. So now there were five of them.

Dad   Mum   Owen   David   Peter

So there they were. But they had no little girl. Then one day Marlene had another baby. This time it was a baby girl. What shall we call our new baby, they said. (They hadn't thought of a girl's name). Then they thought of a beautiful name. It was Alison. So now there were six of them.

Dad   Mum   Owen   David Peter Alison

They all lived in Liverpool or rather a part of Liverpool called Kirkby. They lived at Number 6, Nook Road. But things did not go well, and a sad day came when the children's Mum and Dad could not stay together. Their Dad went away and for a time the children went to stay with some of their Uncles and Aunts. There was Uncle David and Auntie Rose, Uncle Tom and Auntie Mary, and Auntie Joan. Also Auntie Win who lives opposite Uncle David. Then Marlene, their mother, who was always wanting them all to be together, met a boy friend called Ken. She had another little baby girl this time. She was called Christine.

Then came a rather sad time because Marlene became ill. She was very ill and had to go to hospital. So the children had to live with their Uncles and Aunts who were kind to them.

Of course, the children also have a special Grandad and Nana. Grandad is Welsh and proud ot it. They are called Mr. and Mrs. Jones and live in Liverpool.

Their Dad, Roy, said he would look after the children and so all of them, except baby Christine, went to stay with him in a town called Manchester. Christine went to live with Uncle David and Auntie Rose. Here is the house in Manchester where Owen, David, Peter and Alison lived with their Dad:-

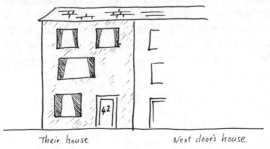

Their house   Next door's house

Now we have to tell you a very sad part of our story. It is about Marlene. I think it is hard to understand why nice people die, but if we believe in God and Jesus then we can also believe that her soul is not dead. But of course it was very sad for her not to get better. The children were sad. Their Mum died in January 1984.

Their Dad got married again. So then the children had a step-mother. Her name was Rachel. She had two children of her own, a boy called Bob and a girl called Barbara.

Owen Dad   Rachel Bob Barbara Alison David Peter

Oh dear, so many children! I'm afraid it did not work, these two familes living together.

Then things got worse. Alison was not at all happy, nor were the boys. After a while their Dad left home and went to Scotland and the children stayed with a friend in Manchester. Their Dad was trying to find work but there was none to be found.

What was going to happen to the three children now? All their Uncles and Aunts had to go to work or they had too many little children to look after. Also, there was a very important person in the family I have not spoken of until now. Here he is:

This is Patch.

Well Peter, David and Alison went to stay with a very nice lady and her family. This lady lived at Number 16 Green Trees Avenue, Sale. her name was Sylvia Brown. The children called her Auntie Sylvia. Also there was Mr. Brown who was called Will. He worked in Manchester. They had three children: June, who was nearly grown up because she was fourteen; Graham, a big boy who was twelve; and Kath who was nine. here is the house in Sale:

The children went here but the social worker said she didn't know how long they would be there because Mrs. brown usually took children for a short time.

Of course this meant going to a new school as well and meeting lots of new people, and this is not easy to do. Sometimes the children thought about their Mum and Dad.

A few times their Dad arranged to see them at the social worker's office. The social worker was Miss Southdene. Owen had gone to live with Auntie Mary and Uncle Tom, and so had Patch the cat.

Then something happened rather quickly. So quickly that it was rather a shock for the children. Will Brown, their short-term foster father, was told by his boss at work that he would have to move and go and live miles away. It was not possible for the children to go with the Brown family so they would have to move.

Oh dear, said David. Oh dear, said Peter. Oh, oh dear, said Alison and she started to cry. Of course they were upset again as they did not know who they would have to look after them, and their Dad had disappeared.

But one day, Miss Southdene brought a very nice lady and gentleman to see them. The gentleman was called John Gillmoss, and the lady was Betty Gillmoss. At first the children were a bit shy and were a bit worried as they didn't know John and Betty. But after a bit they found that they were ever so friendly and seemed very kind! So they showed them their toys.

Then, in the middle of the summer, came the big move when all three children went to live with Mr. and Mrs. Gillmoss. Miss Southdene said she did not think they would stay with Betty and John for a long time, only about six months, which is as long as halfway between one birthday and the next.

Betty and John have some children of their own, but they were all much bigger even than David. They have two boys who are about eleven years old and two very big girls. The boys are called Sam and Jonathan, and the grown-up girls are called Rebecca and Susan:-

Alison   John   Betty   Rebecca   Susan   David   Peter   Sam   Jonathan

They all live in a super house in a place called Cheadle.

Now the children must also think about the future.

One day, just before Christmas, Miss Southdene the social worker, brought a new social worker to meet the children. His name is Mr. Ken

Redgrave. This is him:-

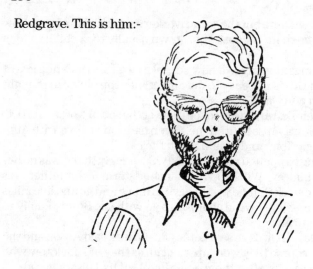

We will tell you the rest of this story later on.

APPENDIX B

Check List on Preparation

Question re: task or condition	Extension of Question	Further Comments
SET 'A' Readiness expressed by or observed in the child.	SET 'A'	SET 'A'
1. Is the child able with help to adjust satisfactorily to the loss of old parenting ties?	This can be extended to less of other ties such as siblings. A positive answer implies a degree of trust in the future caregiver's willingness to accept him.	It need not be that the child has resolved the loss completely. This may take several years. But the worker must know that the child has had an opportunity to come to terms and is likely to be able to deal with the new relationships pending, without unresolved problems of this nature inhibiting the relationship unduly.
2. Is the child able to accept a new parenting relationship.		The question is obviously a pair question with the one above. However it raises several subsidiary questions and could be linked to anxieties resulting from previously disrupted fostering and other relationships.
3. Is the child able to accept a new, or a first ever sibling relationship.		

Question re: task or condition	Extension of Question	Further Comments
4. Does the child show a satisfactory degree of being able, intellectually and emotionally, to accept the facts about the practical possibility or impossibility of returned to previous caregivers?		This also pair with Question No. 1 but we have in mind here the sort of situation in which the child needs help in accepting some administrative factor causing separation, e.g. both parents on a 'life' sentence. Again, we cannot expect emotional problems to go. We are more concerned with the child's ability, with help, to handle them.
5. Has the child expressed sufficiently strongly and without pressure a wish to be placed in the type of placement in ming?	i.e. Does the child want to be fostered, or adopted? Does he like the idea of going to live with his uncle and aunt?	Obviously the answers must, to some extent, relate to the age and ability of the child. Some children have first-hand knowledge of fostering. Some could not be expected to understand. But a young child will talk about a new Mum and Dad.
6. With older children in the case of a plan for adoption, has the child been explicit enough in showing a wish for this?	Does the child understand sufficiently what is meant by legal adoption.	The age of the child must count here, as the intellectual development. It is up to the worker and the potential adopters to be intellectually honest if they know the child is able to understand.

Question re: task or condition	Extension of Question	Further Comments
SET 'B' tasks in direct work with the child.	SET 'B'	SET 'B'
7. Have the questions in column two been dealt with sufficiently with the child?	Most of the children need answers to these questions: Who am I? To whom do I belong? What is going to happen to me?	Although I have reduced these questions to simple little sentences such as 'Who am I?' the reader will appreciate that we may be talking of months of work helping a child to establish a more satisfying sense of identity.
8 .Has the child had sufficient opportunity to review his own history?	And has he used it to make adjustments or to gain new perceptions?	The 'opportunities' will include 'Life Story Books', photographs, visits, Birth Certificates, etc. and discussion round these things.
9. Have the child's *feelings* concerning people and events in his history been brought out and coped with?		This is delicate area and skill and understanding is required so as not to probe just for the sake of probing.
10. Has work been undertaken with the child to establish any emotional 'blockage'.	Has it been possible to help the child (to unblock?) sufficiently for placement to proceed?	Again, provided the emotional blocks will not adversely affect the placement it is far better for the healing to take place, and more likely, within a developing attachment/bonding matrix.

160

Question re: task or condition	Extension of Question	Further Comments
11. Has work been undertaken with the child to establish the level of *emotional* development?	This question concerns the emotional/social development. Arnold Gessell's work is helpful in assessing levels. Treatment may include taking the child through regression therapy.	*Development* will take place within a satisfactory attachment/ bonding matrix but it is essential that caregivers know at what level the child is func tioning when he first joins them, and how to relate to him.
12. Has the child been helped to mourn the loss of any attachment figures.		
SET 'C' Assessment and information obtained from documentation, other professionals, family, etc.	SET 'C'	SET 'C'
13. Has an assessment of the child's development, and the stages he is functioning at been made?	Includes: emotional/social, emotional barriers, physical intelligence (academic level, etc), and moral understanding or 'conscience' development?	This information should be obtained early and before beginning any in-depth direct working with the child.
14. Has the worker obtained a true-as-possible and detailed-as-possible history of the child?	This will be obtained from various sources (official and otherwise) but it must not be overlooked that the child may often be the only one holding factual information.	It is advisable for the worker to make a detailed flow chart of the child's history before commencing direct work.

Question re: task or condition	Extension of Question	Further Comments
15. Has a study been made concerning the child's present and previous attachment figures?		Unless the worker is aware of such people in the child's life it is possible that other questions set above will not be sufficiently covered.
16. Has an assessment been made concerning the extent to which the child's self-image (self-identity) or ego may have been adversely affected?		The degree to which this aspect is assessed or investigated will depend on a number of factors. Many children will not require a full assessment made by a psychologist, or other specialist, others will.
17. Has an assessment been made to establish whether there are important areas of missing life experiences?		These may be the seemingly 'small' things in life like never having seen the sea! Or much more important self-identity areas such as the child who has missed 'being a child' because she had to take charge of things from a very tender age.
18. Has an assessment been made to establish any areas of mis-perception of an ontological nature?	Some children who have 'missed out' or been unable to relate in a normal way find it hard to understand aspects of time, space, sound, etc.	

Question re: task or condition	Extension of Question	Further Comments
SET 'D' Tasks which the care agency must ensure have been undertaken.	SET 'D'	SET 'D'
19. Has the preparation work taken account of the views of other workers and people in touch with the child?	This includes specialists such as psychiatrists, psychologists. Also field and residential social workers, teachers, medical people, members of the child's family and others who are or should be involved.	Of course, if other specialists are involved the whole process should be a team undertaking, and an early decision has to be taken concerning 'key' workers and who will undertake the direct work with the child.
20. Has a profile of the child's behavioural adaptions been made?	This includes aggressive behaviour, withdrawn behaviour, 'telling lies', stealing, sexual behaviour, etc.	Some interpretation of the psychosocial 'goal', and also the aeteology and onset will be helpful. This information helps the worker to deal with other tasks referred to above. By psychosocial 'goal' is meant the subconscious motivation or indeed the conscious social motivation.

REFERENCES

CURTIS, P. (1983 'Involving Children in the Placement Process' in: *Adoption and Fostering,* Vol. 7. No. 1. British Agencies for Adoption and Fostering.

DONLEY, K. (1975) *Opening New Doors,* British Agencies for Adoption and Fostering.

DREIKURS, R. (1965) 'Music Therapy' in: *Conflict in the Classroom: The Education of Emotionally Disturbed Children,* Long N.J. et (eds.) Wadworth.

FAHLBERG, V. (1981) *Helping Children When They Must Move,* British Agencies for Adoption and Fostering.

'FAMILYMAKERS' (1983) *Finding Out About Me,* Catholic Children's Society, 49 Russell Hill Road, Purley, Surrey, U.K.

FITZGERALD, J. et al., (1982) *Building New Families,* Basil Blackwell, Oxford, U.K.

FITZGERALD, J. (1983) *Understanding Disruption,* British Agencies for Adoption and Fostering.

GAUSSEN, T. (1984) 'Developmental Milestones or Conceptual Millstones?' in: *Child Care, Health and Development.* Vol. 10. No. 2.

GOFFMAN, E. (1963) *Stigma: Notes on the Management of Spoiled Identity,* Prentice Hall.

KADUSHIN, A. (1960) *Adopting Older Children,* Columbia University Press.

LOWENFELD, M. (1979) *The World Technique,* Allen and Unwin.

McCOLLUM, J.A.   (1984) 'Social Interaction Between Parents and Babies: Validation of an Intervention procedure' in: *Child Care, Health and Development.* Vol. 10. No. 5. Blackwell Publications.

MORRIS, J.   (1987) (Child Care Consultant) in a paper read to Assoc. for Child Psychology and Psychiatry: 'Re-Alerting the Senses': A Pathway Back to Emotional Growth', Manchester, U.K.

OAKLANDER, V.   (1978) *Windows to our Children,* Real People Press.

OWEN, P. and CURTIS, P.   (1983) *Techniques for Working with Children, No. 1.* (Photocopy) Owen and Curtis, 59 Cedar Ave., Euxton, Chorley, Lancs.

RYAN, T. and WALKER, R.   (1985) *Making Life Story Books,* for Adoption and Fostering.

SAWBRIDGE, P.   (1983) *Parents for Children,* British Agencies for Adoption and Fostering.

THOM, M.   (1984) 'Working with Children: The Violet Oaklander Approach' in *Adoption and Fostering.* Vol. 8. No. 3.

TRISELIOTIS, J.   (1983) 'Identity and Security' in: *Adoption and Fostering.* Vol. 7. No. 1.

WINNICOTT, C.   (1964) *Child Care and Social Work,* Caldicote Press.

DISCUSSION SLIDERS
THREE TYPICAL SLIDERS

Favourite Things Happy Things	Scarey Things? Things I Worry Over — Maybe?	How I Feel Or Think
Favourite hits	Mum being ill	Pleased
Favourite stars	Illness	Happy
Favourite games	Crying	Nice
Things I'd like to do	Being sad	Great
Favourite dreams	School	Beautiful
I want to	Dreams	Love it
I also want to	Being afraid	Foolish
I love	Feelings inside me	Strange
and	Things I can't talk about	Silly
and	Sad things	Naughty
	Things I might do	Sad
	Other things	Cross
		Upset
		Annoyed
		Worried
		Afraid
		Angry
		Spiteful
		Hate it
		Jealous